EMPIRE-BUILDING
by Writing and Speaking

A How-To Guide
For Communicators,
Entrepreneurs, and Other
Information Merchants

by Gordon Burgett

Also written by Gordon Burgett

Query Letters/Cover Letters
Speaking For Money (with Mike Frank)
How To Sell 75% of Your Freelance Writing
Ten Sales From One Article Idea
The Query Book

Empire-Building by Writing and Speaking: For Communicators, Entrepreneurs, and Other Information Merchants, by Gordon Burgett. Printed and bound in the United States of America. All rights reserved. No part of this book may be reproduced in any form or by any electronic or mechanical means including information storage and retrieval systems without permission in writing from the publisher, except by a reviewer who may quote brief passages in a review. Published by Communication Unlimited, P.O. Box 1001, Carpinteria, CA 93013. First edition.

Copyright © 1987 by Gordon L. Burgett

Library of Congress Catalog Card Number: 87-070341

ISBN 0-910167-03-6 (hardcover)

ISBN 0-910167-02-8 (paperback)

Copies may be ordered directly from the publisher for $12.95 (paperback) or $15.95 (hardcover) plus $1 for postage and handling. (California residents add 6% for state sales tax.) For terms on volume quantities, please contact the publisher.

Special appreciation to
Patricia Allaback, for editorial assistance
Paul Fraser, for cover design

Preface

A running friend asked me what the "empire" in empire-building meant and I didn't know how to reply to him. I still can't answer that properly. But "empire" is the right word with which to begin the title of this book.

You see, I believe that each of us knows something that others want to know or should know.

What you know, or could, is the seed of your empire.

And you share that kind of knowledge through writing and speaking, thus the second part of this book's title.

It's through those tools that you create and control your empire; you become the emperor or the empress.

In one sense your empire is like a bountiful tree that grows from that single seed of knowledge. For knowledge has its roots in all other knowledge, from common soil. Yet each tree stands alone, a singular masterpiece, flowering and feeding and providing shade. And pollinating, begetting more knowledge, more seeds, more empires . . .

In another way, your empire means freedom and power and money and control. It means creation, the taking of one idea or one cell of information and building from it, in the best way, a kingdom where you, the builder, have done the building and earned the rewards for daring, tenacity, faith, and hard work.

So I have difficulty describing one's empire in universal terms, for the empire is as much the person as the deed, with as much variation as the genes of the doer and the elements of what is done.

The process, on the other hand, is easier to tell. You define an idea, put it in the center, and build outward. Through the means of idea or information dissemination — articles, books, seminars, speeches, tapes, consulting, newsletters, film, and many more — you work from the core of that idea to its farthest reach, as you build from a drop of rain a sea.

This book explains the process, then shows it in motion through an example.

For twenty years I have experimented with the means that this book describes, and have written and spoken much about them. Along the way my own tiny empire has emerged. It took the full twenty years to build. Had a book of this kind existed it would have taken about three.

On the other hand, without those extra seventeen years of doing almost everything wrong, and learning by trying to get it right, I could not have written these pages.

But there's no reason why you too should lose that time just to rediscover the same or a similar process. Your time is too valuable, your idea too special, your information too needed. So take from these pages what gets you quickly to your core, then build and share so we all may benefit.

Some of the ideas suggested will be new, and the reading slow. I've opted to give a variety of examples, to expand the breadth of the concept. That too can confuse. Just keep the title in mind: empire-building by writing and speaking. All the roads travelled, suggested, or hinted at go the same direction, and the rewards can be well worth the extra mental mileage. Keep going . . .

Empire-building by writing and speaking works if you do. In this world emperors and empresses build their own empires. You can do it too.

Dedication

To my my father, *James William Virgil Burgett,*
who died while this book was being written.
A kind, courageous, feisty friend who knew how to laugh.

and to Jean and Mom, whom he loved and loved him,

and to those of you who loved him too,
or would have had you known him.

Contents

PART FIVE: Assorted Guides

PART
ONE

Knowing The Path

Thoughts and suggestions. . .

Organizing an Idea

There is a simple way to organize any idea for dissemination through a seminar, speech, article, or book.

First, note what you want to share about that idea. Be sure to include the needs your idea meets and the benefits people gain by knowing it.

Second, from your collected thoughts about the idea, write in one sentence the purpose of your oral or written presentation.

Third, change that purpose statement into a question.

Fourth, list the questions that logically emanate or flow from your question. Use the prompters — what, where, when, who, why, and how — and add other questions specific to the topic. These questions become the segments of your seminar, the elements of your speech, the parts of your article, or the chapters of your book. Starting from the core of your purpose, they keep you on track and logically organized.

For example, a good purpose statement for an article might be, "This article will show how to train for the ultramarathon." The working question might then be "How does one train for an ultramarathon?" Secondary questions, and thus sub-topics in the article, might be (1) what is an ultramarathon and what constitutes proper training for it? (2) where could one train? (3) when could one expect to actually begin participation? (4) who could participate in an ultramarathon — physically, emotionally, economically? (5) why would anyone want to, and (6) how could one train, from the first day until the final event?

Each secondary question, in turn, suggests further questions, which continue the organization from the general topic to the specific details. The answers to those questions? Those are the words that form a logically organized talk or text!

Source: *Writing and Speaking Your Idea Into a Windfall*

Fifteen Steps To Empire-Building by Writing and Speaking

1. List the major goals you wish to achieve.

2. Select those that can be achieved through information dissemination.

3. List your present economic needs, then predict those needs in one, two, and three years.

4. List your resources — present, anticipated, and potential — then predict those resources in one, two, and three years.

5. From the goals you can achieve through information dissemination, determine which could meet your economic needs, then select from them the one you most want to achieve.

6. State that goal as an objective, clearly define it, identify its core subject, formulate a purpose statement from it, and convert that into a working question.

7. Explain why you want to pursue that objective.

8. Research the core subject: definition, facts, resources, references, needs, state of the art.

9. Determine the benefits and those most benefitted by the realization of your objective.

10. Explore fully the ways by which you could develop and market your core subject through information dissemination means.

    a. Sub-topic pad.
    b. Grid.
    c. Working and secondary questions.
    d. Asking around. . .
    e. Topic-spoking.
    f. More topic-spoking.
    g. Topic-tiering.

11. Develop action paths that would lead to the realization of your objective.

12. Specify the markets that would best bring the benefits of your objective to the beneficiaries.

13. Create, prioritize, and time-sequence an action plan that would lead to the realization of your objective.

14. Implement your action plan.

15. Review your objective, means, and implementation.

"The tongue is the mind's messenger"

Bahya Ibn Paquda (1050-1120), *Duties of the Heart*

"Success depends on three things: who says it, what he says, how he says it; and of these three things, what he says is the least important."

John, Viscount Morley of Blackburn, *Recollections*, 1917

PART
TWO

Knowing Yourself

Thoughts and suggestions. . .

Ideas

Ideas *per se* the most important element to getting into print. Almost any idea written well enough and marketed with tenacity could find lodging on some page — if you don't care where, how much you receive for your labors, or how long its preparation or placement takes.

Those in print often and profitably match ideas to the readers' greatest needs and brightest dreams.

Source: *How To Sell 75% of Your Freelance Writing*

———————————————

"No star in today's educational sky shines brighter nor is any form of idea dissemination easier to enter. You need neither a degree nor a pedigree, just knowledge that others need to know; the skill and integrity to share it fully, honestly, and clearly; and the courage to do so openly in the market place."

Source: *Speaking For Money*

1

"WHAT DO I WANT TO DO WITH MY LIFE?"

"What do I want to do with my life?"

"How do I want to be remembered?"

"What kind of contribution do I want to leave?"

Those may be the kinds of questions you have been asking yourself. Big questions. Your future at stake.

Yet no book can answer those questions equally well for every reader, if it can really answer them at all. Rather, this book will suggest ways that you might answer them for yourself, with a process and some thought patterns that could help put your life on such a path of long-term meaning.

Empire-Building by Writing and Speaking begins by asking you to make a list.

Active, bright people like you have no trouble listing "things" to which they want to dedicate their lives — projects, causes, plans, and dreams worthy of your days.

You may envision a world saved by your word. Or running the Super Bowl TD in overtime. Or a cancer cure, schizophrenia vanquished, free fuels — nothing is beyond the fecund mind of man. And if one, why not all?

Alas, that describes the problem as well as the vision(s): to achieve it, or them, takes more than a few words on a list. It takes dedication, hard work, organization, even skills.

Dedication — the singleminded, no-nonsense variety that breeds success — needs one purpose to realize, steps to follow, and means by which to attain and measure that realization. One purpose, one objective. One clear, irridescent goal at which all the physical and mental toil, the energy, and the hope can be directed. Too many goals are like too many chefs: the souffle ends up a murky stew.

Which is not to say that you are limited to one goal a lifetime, nor that your goals must be earthsaving in aim.

Just meeting daily needs is one kind of goal; food, shelter, and security are needs of the first order that must be met before one can seriously consider empire-building.

The exceptional people who read this book and want to do more than merely exist and satisfy those basic needs will have many goals. Empire-building suggests a way to turn those many dreams into reality.

Later you will be asked to reduce your goals, beyond meeting your basic needs, to one.

The first step, now, is to list every hope, dream, desire, idea, or goal in which you fully believe and to which you want to focus your energy and skills. Anything you would like to do to better life. Any wrong you want to help right. Any need you want to help meet. Add them to your list. That list can never be too long, unless the process of list-making becomes an excuse for progressing no further.

State each item in sentence form, beginning with "I want to ...." That will force you to further define each goal, to give it a logical form. Some ideas melt in that much sunlight. Others gain a new clarity.

It is *your* list. You needn't share it. Make it as long as your convictions and dreams dictate.

But put all your ideas down. Fantasies are free at step one! It's your life, your dreams, your paper. Take your time — but not too much time!

EXAMPLE

If you're like me, you can grasp and remember a new concept much better and faster when it's related to your own life or when you can see it demonstrated by somebody else.

So what we need is a model through which we can better comprehend the new concepts of empire-building by writing and speaking.

My life would be an inappropriate model. My wee empire was in fact built from writing and speaking, but the concepts came to me after-the-fact. This book proposes that you get there intentionally — and much quicker! So I'm the wrong person.

And I know too little about you.

So let's create a new you. Let's focus on an idea we can all relate to, put you there, and develop each of the fifteen steps of the empire-building process around you.

If you'll lend me a bit of your imagination and some patience, the reward should be an easy-to-grasp base from which later, with modest modification, you could more quickly and surely build your own empire.

Congratulations, you are now in your mid-40's! Familiar terrain? A blissful leap backward? Or dreaded, instant aging?

Even worse, if there is worse, you are also a neuter: it doesn't matter if you're male or female! Except that you must be one or the other since you have two children, a daughter in college and a son who, from threats and appearance, may be the first permanent member of the high school junior class!

Why the mid-40's? That's a time when many become driven by a desire to do something with their own specialness. They have also acquired some knowledge and skills, have access to sufficient starting capital to try something new, and have heard the first loud ticking of the mortal clock.

Some so driven are motivated to bolt from the pack by an idea that simply must be shared. Or by a need to prove their worth. Some want the rewards that singular success can bring: wealth, acclaim, options. Others want to leave something of themselves to be admired by their grand-childrens' grandchildren. Most want all of those things plus more. As do you in our example.

The first step of the fifteen requires you to list the things that you very much want to do with what remains of your life. Major goals, which sometimes in the listing don't look quite that major. But they are to you.

So let's give you nine such goals, stated in first-person as such a list must always be done:

1. I want to start riding my 10-speed cycle, with a light pack and minimal sleeping gear, to see the world, stopping when and where I wish, expenses paid, no cares, for a week, a year, or forever.
2. I want to play with the Chicago Cubs. Pitch, preferably, or catch. Hit .300 and help them win the pennant — repeatedly.
3. I want to write a novel about the *sertão* area of northeastern Brazil, to show how similar people are despite widely divergent cultures and levels of material well-being.
4. I want to write a series of academic papers, then a book comparing the religious sects begun in the U.S. with others founded elsewhere during the same historical period.
5. I want to establish a nationwide "run-your-age" program for marathoners and others seeking a new level of achievement.
6. I want to show writers how and why to self-publish their books.
7. I want to invent a method to flange aluminum tubing.
8. I want to develop a program that will enlist the best qualities of every human being in the creation of a "perfect human world."
9. I want to patent a nutritive, edible grain that will thrive on heat and grow in sand.

That's your list. It's an ambitious assortment of goals and dreams. We'll look at each of the nine in the next step!

(So much for your exemplary self. And for this kind of follow-up note. What the example does, chapter-by-chapter, you are to do, in a similar fashion, for your own empire. If the nine points above are in fact precisely what you want your empire to do, this book is a miraculous bargain! But if your true goals are different, list each beginning with "I want to ...." Don't abbreviate your list. There are hundreds of causes, thousands of ideas that need definition, direction, and tenacious energy. The bedrock of your empire and the basis of your being praised by those grandchildrens' grandchildren may be number 23 on your list. Pity if you stopped listing — to kick back and have a beer — at 22!)

"Knowledge is a hoard from which nothing can be lost."

Ibn Gabirol (1021-about 1058)

2

Information Dissemination Means

Those seeking guidance in this book have chosen particular ways by which they plan to realize their goals: through writing and speaking. But which of their listed goals are actually realizable by these means?

Writing and speaking are the primary means of information dissemination. Yet writing for a purpose is more than an endless outpouring of words and sentences. It is done in comprehensible forms. The same is true of speaking, and at times the two are combined to better disseminate information in still other, purposeful ways.

What are these ways and forms? Which are the most commonly used means of information dissemination?

In *writing*, probably articles, newsletters, reports, and books.

In *speaking*, talks, speeches, seminars, classes, and audio cassettes.

While *both* are used in consulting, as well as in video cassettes and film.

Your task is to see which of the goals listed in Step One lend themselves to being fully developed through writing and speaking. Further, if we understand an empire as being income-generating and, ultimately, self-sustaining, the goals must also generate income, and enough of it, by those means.

Most likely some of the goals on your list won't qualify. Which doesn't mean that they are less worthy or that they can't or shouldn't be pursued. It simply means that if you presently wish to focus on writing or speaking, or both, to realize a goal, this isn't their hour.

EXAMPLE

Which of your nine goals could be realized by writing and speaking?

The first goal, the cycling escape, might lend itself to articles and a book, and you might be able to sing for your gruel (as a somewhat melodic form of speaking) if the listeners were particularly music-starved and indiscriminate, but the "no cares" element removes it from this form of development. To survive and build an empire you'd have to care. Desperately, if singing was to be part of the income-earning!

Playing with the Chicago Cubs is a true fantasy for more than a couple dozen lucky lads. Off the list, with regrets.

Three and four, the novel about the *sertão* and the papers/book about religious sects, remain. Plunk in the center of writing/speaking.

Establishing a "run-your-age" program isn't as easy to categorize. Some of the early promotional steps could be done through articles, and the idea could be further spread through a book, speaking to groups, on radio and TV talk shows, and so on. Yet the essence of the concept isn't one of communication, other than the idea. It's an event, or many. A physical thing, with sponsors, release forms, "sag wagons," certificates, and miles more — many, many running miles more. In summary, out.

Of all, (6) "showing writers how and why to self-publish their books," lends itself best to the means of information dissemination.

Inventing a way to flange aluminum tubing hasn't a thing to do with writing or speaking. Not for this list!

Conversely, the "perfect human world" is basically a concept, with many how-to's, that starts from information dissemination and ends with the kind of world we scarcely dare to dream of. It stays.

And the grain that grows in sand: lab stuff, germinations less of the keyboard or tongue than of air, water, and soil. Deleted, for now.

What's left? Still in the running are (3), (4), (6), and (8).

(I fibbed. A last reminder: do the same for your list. Evaluate and eliminate.)

3

Needs

I n Step Three a different kind of list is required: of your economic needs, both life-sustaining and life-enhancing.

Some needs are more desirable than essential, like BMWs and electric toothbrushes. Others are critical to survival, or at least to maintaining a minimally acceptable quality of life, like food, clothing, shelter, security, transportation, education, and health. Focus on the latter here. There will be plenty of time for the frills when the empire is up and flourishing!

Life-sustaining needs change very little over the years, other than by an increase or decrease in the size of the family or its members. But life-enhancing needs, beyond bare survival, do vary, and with inflation and outside forces affecting the dollar value of those needs, your list won't remain static or constant.

Therefore, because you don't know at what point your empire will be able to fully meet those needs, you should also predict your needs one, two, and three years from now.

EXAMPLE

Since you have a family and are in your 40's, let's further presume that you have a job and can remain at it until its income can be replaced by your empire's earnings.

Here you must list your needs for the first year, then the second and third, by which time your empire should be in full function and picking up the tab.

What might those needs be?

1. To meet food, mortgage, insurance, and basic home and family costs: a guesstimate of $35,000/yr.
2. To help pay costs for your daughter in college (in addition to federal/state aid): $2,600/yr.
3. To replace your second car (with its failing engine): $6,500 for a pick-up truck with a shell, to be used for home and the new business.
4. To pay the deductible on health/car insurance: $650, average needed the past two years.
5. To pay anticipated sports-related costs for your son in high school: $250/yr.
6. To buy a computer and basic office equipment for the new business: $2,800.
7. For other new business costs unmet by income: $1,500, first year; $2,500, second year; $5,000, the third.

Thus, to meet your needs will cost about $42,000 the first year, if you buy the truck and computer/office equipment with a deposit and installments. That will rise to about $43,000 the second year. The third? Less than $50,000.

Too modest? Too much? Put in your own numbers. You have to start somewhere.

"There is only one success — to be able to spend your life in your own way."

Christopher Morley, *Where the Blue Begins*, 1922

"The man who does not make a choice makes a choice."

Jewish folk saying

4

Resources

Nobody creates an instant empire.

Your idea might bring quick returns, you might live on the income while you construct an imperial structure, and all of this listing of goals and needs might, in retrospect, seem foolish.

But even quick success would be the rare exception. Like most businesses, empire-building by writing and speaking takes time, the initial returns are modest, and there is risk.

So you must survive between the point at which you select your goal and it becomes fully realized. Careful planning can help you buy the time necessary for your idea to grow.

That's where your present, anticipated, and potential resources come into play, and why your task now is to create a third list of them, as they are now and as they might be in a year, two, and three.

Empire-building is generally done with four variables: a goal, your desire and hard work, income from another job, and additional resources. You are in the process of defining the goal; desire and hard work are constants. Other income and additional resources are what you list here.

When the empire produces sufficient income to meet its and your needs, you won't require the other income nor will it be necessary to dip into additional resources. But in the meantime you must know how much other income you can expect and what additional resources can be called upon to meet those needs.

Successful emperors and empresses make lists. Trust me. The last thing we want you to be is listless.

Don't rush. Don't dawdle.

EXAMPLE

At the previous step we saw that it would cost between $42,000 and $50,000 to survive and launch your empire. Which thrusts you into the typical entrepreneur's dilemma: you need to make money to get going, and you need to get going to make money!

Your question is "How can I build an empire and still know that there will be $42,000 to draw upon for necessities during that first year?"

Follow-up questions must then be, "Where am I going to find that $42,000?" And "When will the empire provide all of the needed capital — plus more?"

Until the empire fully provides, you or somebody else must. Which brings us to the magic word "resources."

What have you saved or cadged for the dire days that you might now tap, as a loan to yourself or an investment for greater returns in the near future? Which of your wealthy relatives recognizes your genius and is begging to invest in it? What delayed earnings or uncollected debts can be converted into operating capital?

Make a list: the resource, from whom it will come, the amount, and when it's accessible.

For our example, you have saved $16,000, which you hope to keep deposited until the second year to earn at least $1,000 more in interest. Thus, at least $17,000 would be available during the second year, $16,000 now.

Second, in your 40's, you have a job at which you earn $48,000 annually. You plan to continue working during the first year, banking the $6,000 above necessities during that time for the second year. You have also accumulated 17 days of sick/bonus leave, in addition to a paid three-week vacation, which you plan to take at the end of the period, freeing you to pursue your goal 38 paid days earlier than might otherwise be possible.

That leaves you $20,000 short for the second year. So you have developed four contingency plans should the income from your empire still be insufficient at that point to pick up the slack:

1. Work part-time for your present employer, or another, as an independent contractor, averaging 20 hours a week times $25/hour, for $14,000.
2. Secure a loan against your whole-life insurance policy for $6,000 or the amount needed.
3. Secure a second or equity loan against your home, now valued at $92,000, with $33,000 still owed, for any part of that $20,000 required, or
4. Continue working for approximately six months longer, full-time, to earn the remaining $20,000 needed for that final period.

We first spoke of three years to develop your empire, but you have resources for two. So your pace must be quicker or your subject, more quickly developed and more quickly income-generating!

Alas, you are covered for two years. During the first year you will be limited to afterwork hours for the empire's development. During the second you hope to have more than half the year free to devote to the empire. If that isn't possible, you should at least have the key hours of the day at your disposal.

"To steer through life on an honest course to the splendors of success — this is a feat reserved for paragons of our kind, a task beyond the nature of the normal man."

Ihara Saikaku (1642-1693), *The Millionaires' Gospel*

"New things succeed, as former things grow old."

Robert Herrick (1591-1674), *Ceremonies for Candlemas Eve*

Thoughts and suggestions. . .

Time

What you sell in the writing world is time, not writing skill. The time to check an idea, query, research, interview, write, edit, submit, and later resell.

If you don't have or develop the writing skill, you simply won't be in print. (But you'll have all that time to do something else just as beneficial and lucrative in another field!)

Source: *How To Sell 75% of Your Freelance Writing*

"A title is the single most important selling tool of a seminar. If the title doesn't make sense, if it doesn't make its reader want to reap the benefits or at least know more about the subject, that person will pick a different seminar — or none at all."

Source: *Speaking For Money*

5

One Goal

Now you must use two of those lists — goals and needs — and set the third aside for later.

You need both lists to select a top goal so that in Step Six you will be able to define it, pinpoint a core subject, and create some valuable working tools.

Your goal list is fat. How do you thin it down? How do you give a comparative value to dreams? The first way is to ask if each goal, if realized, would earn or create sufficient income to meet your needs, partially at first, totally soon after. If not, it must be set aside.

Eliminate dreams that don't draw the dollar? If the empire is to be self-sustaining, if you are to be rewarded on earth in some ratio to the benefits you are bringing others, that is a cruel fact. Empires, at least those with an economic base, aren't built with gossamer or wands.

Goals that might be totally acceptable in another context simply may not be here. If baying at the moon has been your secret wish and greatest dream, bay until you're blue. But moon-baying, like mooning, to my knowledge (since research data is scarce) doesn't pay bills or feed babies. Baying simply isn't empire-building stuff in our context, if any.

You may have to eliminate other goals because they are too imprecise, uncertain, ephemeral, or inappropriate.

The hardest choice comes after the obvious eliminations have been made. If just one goal survives, only two questions remain:

1. Can you build an empire from that goal?
2. Will enough people benefit from it to bring you sufficient income?

But when you must choose from several, assuming that all are of solid empire-building stature and could generate sufficient income, the criteria may be less quantitative. It may get down to which you care the most about, which you most want after your name in the book of contributions, which you will fight the hardest for. Stuff of the heart and guts.

Why just one goal? Why not a dozen jousting for the top nod, each saving the world and filling your till?

Because there is just one you, with your time not unlimited and your energy not boundless. By reducing the number of goals to one now you don't preclude combining other goals or even pursuing different ones later. But you are new to empire-building. You must focus and direct all of your organizational and implementational skills on succeeding with your strongest idea and that which you care the most about.

Too many people spend too much time chasing too many dreams, causes, hopes, and goals. Their lives are a blur, a diffusion. Yours, for maximum effectiveness, for empire-building, must be a penetrating light that flows where you direct it.

I said earlier that dedication — the singleminded, no-nonsense variety that breeds success — needs one purpose to be realized. That means one goal.

It's your empire. You must choose that goal. There will come a night when your more sensible but less singleminded friends are sound asleep and you are left alone with nothing but an idea, a goal between you and defeat or slumber. You had better love that idea like no other. So pick wisely. First with the head, then with the heart.

EXAMPLE

It's time to choose.

Which of the four goals that remained in contention would provide enough earning power at the end of the two years to fully meet your needs? Which even lend themselves to empire-building at all?

We are dealing with guesstimates and exploratory calculations, of course, but often that is enough to eliminate those goals that are clearly inappropriate.

The first goal, to write a novel about the *sertão*, while exciting, wouldn't provide you with enough money, immediately or in two years, to meet your financial needs — nor would it even develop a base for an empire, lest that be more novels which, given enough years and successes, could create such a foundation. (A million-dollar "best-seller"? Maybe. But it makes more sense, if the novel is the goal, to forget the empire now and concentrate fully on producing the best book possible, and if it proves wildly successful, later build the empire around the book or topic.)

The second goal, academic papers, then a book, comparing religious sects, is as intellectually intriguing as the first, but as questionable in terms of commercial success or appropriateness for a financially self-sustaining empire. It is more likely the kind of endeavor that validates expertise ideal for an academic career, many unpaid scholarly papers and articles in tightly-focussed journals, books for others interested in the topic, and an occasional invitation to appear on a talk show, free. The kind of empire that can enlighten mankind and satisfy the soul but lacks enough economic power of its own to be considered here.

Simply, the public won't pay much, if anything, to know about either the *sertão* or religious sects because, save in the rarest instance, they have no economic value to them. The primary motivation to read the articles or books, probably in the library, would be curiosity — weak grounds upon which to build an empire.

To show writers how and why to self-publish their books, the third goal, deserves further consideration.

If self-publishing could put the public in print quickly, would be profitable, and the concept could be explained through many means, it looks promising for our kind of empire-building.

The fourth goal might also be good empire-building material: developing a program that would enlist the best qualities of every human being in the creation of a "perfect human world."

Common sense suggests that articles, books, seminars, speeches, and fund-raising could be involved. But when would they produce income?

Tracing the concept's development might provide a tentative answer.

How long would it take to create a comprehensible plan others would support? A year of hard work?

Then how long would it take to get the plan before the public, to create the response and funding necessary for its implementation? Another year or more?

And how long would it take to meet your needs from the meager and scattered financial offerings that a new movement might generate? Who knows — another six months, a year, two?

That's the rub. Nobody knows if the idea will make sense, will attract followers, or will ever generate support. And you have a time plan and resources to feed your family for two only years. Thus the quandry: do you abandon your two-year timetable to keep this fourth goal in consideration?

For the purposes of this book, you do the doable. You have money for two years, so you pass it by for now.

Sounds crass, doesn't it? More power to those who fly in the face of the obviously doable! If you want to achieve your goal hard enough you might find ways to redesign the schedule, move up the income-producing activities, or discover other ways to meet your needs until your empire bears fruit (here, of the mixed-metaphor variety).

But this book takes the safe path: of the four goals only one lends itself to true empire-building within your economic dictates.

Had there been two or more goals still in serious contention, this is where you would have to pick one to pursue, by whatever criteria you wish to use.

It is crucial that at this point the goals be limited to one. Later, that goal can be expanded or other goals can be selected. Now, one battle at a time. Successful generals usually fight many battles. But they are successful because they fight them one at a time, with undivided concentration and all their forces against the same foe.

One battle, one goal: you will show writers how and why to self-publish their books. On to Step Six!

"If I am like someone else, who will be like me?"

Jewish folk saying

"Human history is in essence a history of ideas."

H.G. Wells, *The Outline of History*, 1920

6

Definition

At last, one goal! Which we'll call an objective, to distinguish it from the many unchosen goals still on our list — and others unlisted.

Now you must take that objective and clearly define it so you know precisely, word-by-word, what you want to achieve.

This is done for four reasons, plus common sense.

One, to look with greater clarity at an objective that may have been inexactly or imprecisely phrased when you first listed your many goals in Step One.

Two, to identify its core subject, which will serve as the focal point for research later.

Three, to reduce the definition of that objective to one sentence.

Many contend that if you can't state your objective in terms of your intention and at that length you either have too many objectives posing as one or the purpose is still too vague in your own mind to know what the actual objective is.

In information dissemination, that sentence is known as the "purpose statement." Its implied challenge is usually what drives you, fuels your energy, and directs your promotion; it also acts as a measuring rod for your achievements. So it must be clear and exact. A purpose statement is a powerful working tool.

And four, to convert that one-sentence purpose statement into a "working question," the sub-questions which will later help provide an operating framework for its answer and realization.

Therefore, your energy here is directed at examining the objective, challenging its every word, isolating a core subject, stating (or restating) that objective as a purpose in one sentence, and creating a working question. You also need this level of definition so that, at the next step, you can determine and explain why you want to achieve that precise objective.

Step Six, then, is one of definition. Let's use the example to show the steps and results of definition.

EXAMPLE

You first stated your objective in this way: "I want to show writers how and why to publish their books."

But what specifically does that mean? The first three words are clear enough, but you must question every word that follows.

show: Will you actually "demonstrate"? Do you mean "explain"? Will this vary according to the means used: "show" on video but "explain" on audio cassette? Or perhaps "teach," though that may scare some away?

writers: Do only writers want to self-publish books? Or do all who write books think of themselves as writers? For example, a speaker or an entrepreneur who wants to self-publish is, in one sense, a writer, but may not primarily identify with that classification. And what about the person who acquires a book, or has one ghosted or even written under a different name, and wants to publish it: who is the writer? And would that be self-publishing or just plain publishing? Is it necessary to identify the specific group here? Why not just "people" and let the kind of people come from the context in which the statement is used?

how and **why:** These seem okay, since "how" is the process and "why" the purpose, the key elements others will usually pay to know. The only problem is the order. It's unlikely that others would care to know "how" until they'd been convinced, and that comes from the "why." Why not reverse the order?

to publish: Actually you mean "to self-publish." Except for the possible confusion posed two definitions back, between self-publishing and publishing others' works, you want to distinguish the difference between sending one's written copy to others for them to publish or publishing it oneself. So the term "self-publish" is correct in this context.

their: Again, can a person self-publish others' books? Or by gaining proprietorial rights does it become "their" book? Except for that, the word is proper and to use any other word would be more confusing. But wouldn't it be just as clear if you deleted the word altogether?

books: Two issues — singular or plural, and does one self-publish just books? "Book" presumes that those you will be addressing will write just one. "Books" suggests they need more than one to self-publish or to consider the procedure. And can't one self-publish reports, workbooks, all sorts of printed matter? Even tapes might fall into that category. Again, do you need the word at all?

Yes, this is boring, but if millions are won and lost on periods and commas, as lawyers are quick to say, consider the potential loss from a loose word or three!

The verdict, after much writing of sentences and asking if the new word combinations suggest other confusions, is this:

"I want to show people why and how to self-publish."

Which becomes both your objective and your purpose statement. From it you form your working question, which is simply the heart of the purpose statement put in interrogatory form: "Why should and how can people self-publish?"

From the answer to that question you build your empire.

Thoughts and suggestions. . .

Seminar Subjects: Stick to the Basics

The more basic your seminar subject the easier it will be to attract registrants. If somebody thinks of your topic once a week, approach it with caution. But if they think of it daily, get busy.

People will pay to learn about, improve, control, or enjoy such basics as health, happiness, security, anger, creativity, skills, jobs, recreation, sex, appearance, frustration, loneliness, travel, success, their families . . .

Business is even more predictable. Talk about how to cut losses, how to increase sales or productivity, how to lift morale, or how to instill loyalty or dedication to a product or a boss.

Source: *How To Set Up and Market Your Own Seminar*

"Name recognition doesn't happen because we wish it to. It's the result of persistent marketing and good speaking."

Source: *Speaking For Money*

7

Why Bother?

Empire-building isn't a sometimes, now-and-then, when-you-get-around-to-it thing. Not if you really believe in achieving your objective. And certainly not if you plan to live well from its earnings.

So you must know *why* you want to achieve that objective. Why you are eager to work twice as hard for months and years to attain the goal, what motivates you, what kind of a mark you want to leave. Why you want to contribute so far beyond the normal call of duty. Precisely what do you expect to get from it?

This may be the most difficult of the 15 steps because it asks you to list the precise reasons why you want to sacrifice and double your labors at the possible cost of ridicule and ruin just to convert an objective into reality.

You have already identified the economic needs you must meet during the year or years needed to initiate and establish your empire. Here the questions dig, and the answers dwell, deeper: What of the soul must also be fed? What beyond the tangibles must be there to continually inflame your spirit? What will keep you at the well if the pail starts coming up dry?

Some of the replies will, properly, ring with nobility: you wish to right a wrong, bring equality or justice to the downtrodden, help others realize their fullest potential. Whether these answers are cliches or basic truths, few would object to that kind of motivation.

Yet it's hard for some to admit to less altruistic aims even though many of their more durable drives may come from this less romantic camp: you really want to be loved or admired or respected; you want to be boss; you want money so you can hunt or gamble or wear fancy frills; you want fame; you want to be seen as successful at the thirtieth high school reunion; you want to show the world it was wrong when it said that you wouldn't amount to anything; you want to be a millionaire — oops, billionaire. The list is as long as your imagination, indignation, or ambition. On it are bald, materialistic drives lurking behind the loftier dreams.

Why is this soul-searching necessary? Because the total picture cannot be painted without all of the colors. Life is always in harmony, and to live it fully you too must know, as best you can, what you are seeking and why, to synchronize the harmony of your objective with the greater reality.

Step Seven asks for yet another list, one that states why you want to achieve your objective. A list that ranges from the broadest and loftiest reason to the rawest and narrowest. An honest list of motivators that will keep you empire-building by knowing clearly and embracing firmly all the reasons why.

EXAMPLE

Why, then, do you want "to show people why and how to self-publish"?

For their benefit, for everybody's benefit, and naturally for your benefit. The hard part is figuring out which of them comes first.

Cynically and perhaps even logically, your benefit is probably tops, because if you don't benefit you will have to do something else instead, something that does benefit you enough to meet your needs at every level.

Yet if you don't show others how they can benefit from self-publishing, they won't do it, nobody will benefit (including you), and again you will have to turn elsewhere to meet your needs. A conundrum. The order may be unimportant; perhaps it will sort itself out in the marketing.

Fortunately, this step doesn't require you to make that kind of a choice or determination now. It simply tells you to list the reasons why you want to achieve your objective.

Again, *why* do you want to achieve the objective?

You want "to show people why and how to self-publish" so that, in the process, you will become an acknowledged expert on self-publishing. As an perceived expert you will then

1. be better able to help others put their ideas and words in print
   (a) faster,
   (b) with less risk and more profit,
   (c) with better quality control, and
   (d) on a firmer marketing base than if they did so without the use of your shared knowledge or their confidence in your expertise;
2. be better able to help others gain firmer control of their own means of information dissemination and income generation;
3. be better able to help make available to the world more information and art forms through the new, independently-created publishing;
4. be better able to help bring recognition, through that publishing, to people willing to share their information and publishing skills;
5. have greater personal and professional recognition, contact, and facility in selling products and services about self-publishing, thus increasing your perceived expertise and ability to help others needing that expertise;
6. be more in charge of your own life, responsible for your own well-being, your own development, and the creation and distribution of your own tools of sharing;
7. establish, to extend that sharing, a company that will provide means of offering and distributing related services and products, such as articles, books, speeches, seminars, a newsletter, consulting, etc.,
8. secure, for you, greater financial prosperity and independence;
9. enhance your family's financial security;
10. establish a reputation for yourself and your company that will engender greater pride and benefits for your family and those involved in your endeavors; and,
11. leave, in print and on tape, information useful to others about how they too can enrich themselves and their contemporaries through self-publishing, and as such leave a positive record of your knowledge and existence for the future.

Your objective and the reasons you want to see it achieved are too broad to be met by a single article or an occasional seminar or class. For you to be acknowledged as an expert requires both self-publishing on your part, as evidence that you have done what you teach, and the ability to share the process, at a professional level, with others. That, in turn, requires a campaign and a structure. Which, in our terms, means an empire. On with the building!

PART
THREE

Knowing Your Subject

Thoughts and suggestions...

Query Letters

Query letters open the door to gilded happiness in the free-lancer's writing world. They are your showcase, your business card in full writing flower. They are all the editor knows about you. Learn to do them right. Give them full energy. Invest in them the care and attention to detail you later expect to give the articles you promise.

Source: *How To Sell 75% of Your Freelance Writing*

"As for seminars, there's a desperate need for education in bite-sized proportions. America is full of literate, bright people basically educated but woefully unprepared in the specifics."

Source: *Speaking For Money*

8

Research

Empires, in our context, are built of knowledge which you would provide to others as information — for pay. You would share that commodity through writing or speaking.

Some of that knowledge may be original, the result of studies you have conducted, observations you have made, or experiences you have had or have heard about and from which you have drawn your own conclusions.

Or it may be knowledge accessible to others that you are finding, defining, combining, presenting, or interpreting, where the degree of uniqueness is less a factor than your making it available and understandable.

Sometimes the knowledge is widely known and used and you are making it even more usable by providing a step-by-step process. Or showing how it can be applied either to everyday life or in unusual ways.

Whatever the source or use of the information, the results of your research must be accurate and they must be marketable if you are to build an empire from them.

In terms of accuracy, what you gather and use must be factually correct. Its source(s) must be reliable. Usually, it must also be current.

As for marketability, however it is gathered and packaged, there must be enough people who will buy your information at a sufficiently high price, plus there must be appropriate means to provide and sell it.

Sometimes that information will be so valuable or so constituted that it can be sold by just one means of dissemination. Yet the value of most information can usually be increased many times over by increasing the means of its sale. Later we will see that the use of multiple means can create the bedrock and windfall of your empire.

But for now, what does this mean to you? Research, and plenty of it!

To build an empire from information, you will be expected to understand that information thoroughly, plus much related information leading to and from your point of specialization.

That is, others will expect you to be an expert about your topic. Most of your expertise will come from knowledge already available. Gathering that knowledge; defining it; becoming aware of the references, resources, and future fonts; knowing the "state of the art," and being able to translate what you gather and know into salable information is the purpose of your research. It is also the foundation of your empire and a key to its prosperity.

Where accessible information is located, how it can be obtained, and what more is needed for its best evaluation depends largely upon the topic itself.

Most research for most topics is library-based, then people- and field-found. Add to that personal experience with the applied aspects of the topic and you have covered the main sources.

It is impossible to guess the steps that even typical readers of this book must take to research their empire-building topics. Let me, instead, refer you to your library for books about research techniques, then show you, through the example, how I develop an accurate, comprehensive, current pool of information upon which to build an empire.

As to the length of time your research should take, there are two measurements to consider. Initial, intensive research done at the outset of empire-building may take from 20-100 or more hours of serious application. Assume you know nothing, start from an encyclopedia and other prime points, and move out and toward your specialization.

The second time period lasts as long as your empire exists. You should set aside a specific period of time each week or month for on-going research. Your expertise is as good as today's discovery and tomorrow's investigation. When your learning ends so should your empire.

EXAMPLE

"Self-publishing, why and how." That's the target. Your mission is to find everything written, said, currently under study, and to be said about that topic, both from the theoretical and the applied side.

To that you will add your own experiences with self-publishing. From the total you will, in subsequent steps, design your empire. Your task now is to gather information, like clay, from which the empire can be molded.

Mind you, it would be easy to say, "Hey, you've already self-published many times. Surely you know enough to get by, and you'll learn more . ."

The problem is that you don't know what you don't know. And if you are to be the expert, rather than just a person who knows more than a beginner, you can't count on chance or time to fill in the unknown but critical gaps in your knowledge. You also need a greater view, a wider comprehension of the full field of publishing to see where self-publishing, and your experience with it, fits in. To the task!

The dictionary tells you that "self-" means "by oneself." And "publishing" — the closest is "publish" — has five definitions. "To issue books to the public" is the closest.

A start. You will continue to define the topic until you have all of the meanings in current usage. The encyclopedia tells you more, and cites references. You seek those references out. They expand your knowledge and they cite more references, and the game begins. . .

What do you do with the information you're gathering? Buy four pads of paper. Atop one you write **FACTS**, another, **REFERENCES**, the third, **RESOURCES**, and the fourth, **SUB-TOPICS**. (Some use 3" x 5" index cards instead; I prefer full-length pads of legal paper.)

Every time you find a fact you need to know you put it on your **fact pad**. Yet every fact is not worth recording. How do you decide? Imagine that you will be writing a book about your topic. Everything that should either go into the book or that you will draw upon for related information for the book goes on those pages. (Yes, you'll need many pads of paper or packets of index cards for the facts.)

After each fact you note its source and page number. That's when you tie the fact to your **reference pad**. Rather than write out the same source many times, you note the source once on your reference pad in full bibliographical fashion: author or editor, title, date, and publisher; you also give it a capital letter (A, B, C, etc.). Then on the fact pad every time you note material from that book, article, or printed source, you use the same letter, plus add the specific page number.

Example of a **FACT** pad

```
            FACTS

94% rely on reviews in Library Journal,
  91% - ALA Booklist      - Ⓐ 220
Check to see if prof. assns where you want
   book reviewed have review committees - Ⓑ 127
Send bound galleys to top three: Publishers
Weekly, Library Journal, The Kirkus
Reviews — first reviews needed. Ⓒ 142
```

```
         RESOURCES

TV - Phil Donahue show / L.A. (9-10 A.m.), 2/26/87
Discussing AIDs. Need for good book to trace
the accumulation of knowledge about disease/
public's reaction to knowledge; parallel this to
lack of such widespread info about plague when
it appeared — really a study of communication
and mass psychology.        Ⓘ date above
```

Example of a **RESOURCE** pad

Example of a **REFERENCE** pad

REFERENCES

(A) Poynter, Dan, <u>The Self-Publishing Manual</u>, Sta Barbara, CA: Para Publishing, 3rd ed., 1984.

(B) Shulman, Joel J., <u>How To Get Published in Business/Professional Journals</u>, NY: AMACOM, 1980.

(C) Balkin, Richard. <u>A Writer's Guide to Book Publishing</u>, NY: Hawthorn Books, 1977.

(I) TV/Phil Donahue show — from discussion of panel on 2/26/87

If a fact came from a non-written, generally oral or visual, source — such as an audio or video tape, TV show, speech, or personal interview, — you would also note it on your fact pad, then tie it, in a similar fashion, to your **resource pad**. Who the person is and when the speech was given, where and how you heard it; note anything specific that will help explain and verify the source. As you used capital letters to link written facts to their references, here you use Roman numerals (I, II, III, etc.) on both the fact and resource pads to designate the source. If the fact came from an source that repeats (like a series of programs on television), you should also cite on the pad the specific date on which the fact was heard/seen.

In that way any fact that you think is worth noting can be traced to its source should it be challenged or you later decide to use it in a presentation.

Your **reference pad** may well contain additional information. Should you become aware of or read an article or book that discusses a side issue related to self-publishing but from which, now, you don't wish to extract any facts, you might note that article or book on your reference pad, again in full bibliographical form, and add a sentence or two about it should you wish to use it later.

Likewise, your **resource pad** may well contain more than sources for items beyond the written references.

You may wish to use the second half of your resource pad as a bibliographical font about the top experts whose material you are citing on both your reference and resource pads. Or you may wish to start a fifth pad (I call it the **bio pad**), divided alphabetically into sections. Then every time you encounter biographical information about the key experts on your reference or resource lists, you could add it after their names, with the specific source, using the capital letter or Roman numeral where the information is found. Later, should you need further information about the topic or person, you not only have the expert's name, you may have that person's address, phone number, employer, age, or any other biographical data that will help you find the person quickly or describe him/her more fully for an article or book.

While compiling facts and noting references and resources, on your **sub-topic pad** you note other, related subjects or ideas that stem directly from your topic, that discuss it in a different context, or that might be worth looking at in conjunction with your topic. This pad is where you doodle, play with ideas, make linkages, ask "what if. . .?"

On your sub-topic pad you might list article titles that come to mind.

Or you might develop an outline of self-publishing, attempting to tie the sub-divisions to the main topic in some rational way. Here you might divide the process, for example, into a chronological structure: idea, marketing plan, book research, book writing, early marketing, editing/ proofing, typesetting/illustration/cover preparation, promotion, printing, post-print marketing, distribution, long-range marketing.

Or a half-dozen or more other kinds of structuring: developmental, historical, legal, financial, integrational (where self-publishing is part of a greater publishing plan), or imperial (where self-publishing is part of a multi-media empire, as we are describing in this book).

Why bother? Because you want to understand the relationship between the parts of self-publishing when and as they funtion together. This pad gives depth and a third dimension to the topic that must be understood to be able to relate fully to all or any of the parts.

Where do you find the material to put on these pads?

The library first, then people, then the field. Alas, it's not quite that easy — nor that cleanly divided.

In the library, after consulting the dictionary and encyclopedia, you note the references cited and check the card catalog. It tells you the books, microfiche, microfilm, and the cross-references you must check to find more related material. You write down the reference numbers of the items in the card catalog, then head to the stacks, to review the material at hand, including other items stacked nearby that might also discuss self-publishing.

Bibliographies are the researcher's godsend. Using another's compilation of available references, often with an evaluation of each, greatly simplifies the hunt. Fortunately, in self-publishing John Kremer's *The Independent Publisher's Bookshelf* does just that. Better yet, it's comprehensive and reliable. It reduces the gap you must fill to all that has appeared in print between its preparation and now.

Then check the *Reader's Guide to Periodical Literature* to see what articles not in the bibliography have been published about the topic, working backward from the most recent listing for at least ten years. Not only will you discover the magazines most interested in self-publishing, you'll find more cross-references.

In some fields there is an academic index much like the *Reader's Guide* that list as many, or more, different articles about the topic, plus the publications interested in it. Alas, that is not the case with self-publishing. You check the closest, *The Business Index*, and find a few listings.

Are there magazines or trade journals that contain information about your topic? You can approach this in three ways: (1) the periodicals listing at the library (which sometimes includes an even larger listing if that library, say, is part of a state university system or commonly held or cross-listed confederation), (2) the trade directories for publishers or self-publishers, and (3) the current *Writer's Market* which contains information for writers wishing to submit to some 4,000 publications.

Once more, if you find publications of interest in any of those sources, you note them, check the *Reader's Guide* and the academic indexes to see if their contents are included, and if not, you seek the annual indexes to see what has appeared on their pages about self-publishing. Finally, you find the specific articles you want to review.

By searching so thoroughly you are doing more than gathering material for your own information, you're collecting a list of the publications most likely to use your articles about self-publishing should that be an avenue by which you share and advertise your expertise. Also, should you decide at some later date to have a book about the topic published by another publisher (what a heretical thought!), the publishers you have listed in your book references will be those most likely to be interested in publishing your tome.

Another source of information are newspaper indexes of the larger newspapers in the United States and England.

Newsletters about self-publishing, or writing in fields where self-publishing is common, should be excellent fonts of current information. A good listing of newsletters, *The Oxbridge Directory of Newsletters*, will lead you to those presently in print. (Many newsletters will also send a complimentary copy so you can decide whether to include them in your personal library.)

Professional groups, like Publishers Marketing Association (P.M.A.) or COSMEP, have their own newsletters plus directories of members, most of whom are self-publishers. Your librarian can lead you to the directories of associations. Plugging into that membership and attending meetings will open up many more opportunities to explore the field, find out about the most useful newsletters and publications, meet successful practitioners, and see who else in the field has built an empire around the topic, how extensive it is, and whether there is room for you and them.

Joining such groups and appearing on their mailing lists quickly subjects you to advertising for related seminars, workshops, classes, conferences, and products new and/or necessary to the trade. That, in turn, can quickly expand your "insider's expertise."

Most of your facts about the state of the art will come from those sources or the rare article about this theme, as well as from discussions with people on the front edge of the new technology and marketing techniques. They will also be the people most likely to know who is doing the current research or experimentation — and where self-publishing is headed in the future.

Information is vital to empire-building: the more of it you have, the more options you have available. But now we must convert this information into empire-building blocks.

Any empire of lasting substance needs lots of clay of reliable quality. Clay to rework into enduring blocks from which an empire can be built. Keep digging.

"In this game you have to be a finisher. I call it "finishing," and you don't learn it in Miss Hewitt's school for young ladies."

Archie Moore, boxing champion, 1961

"I never practice, I always play."

Wanda Landowska, master harpsichordist, 1952

"Whoever is able to write a book and does not, is as if he has lost a child."

Nachman of Bratslav (1770-1811)

Thoughts and suggestions. . .

"There are speakers talking about self-esteem who have extremely low self-esteem. And others talking about successful sales skills who were dismal failures as salespeople, or are terribly unprofessional in selling their services as a speaker. The danger is obvious. Sooner or later the difference will catch up with them."

Source: *Speaking For Money*

Rights

Some won't send their writing or their ideas for publication because they think they will be stolen.

Don't worry about rights in the beginning. Worry about writing something worth stealing, then sell it.

Source: *How To Sell 75% of Your Freelance Writing*

9

Benefits and Beneficiaries

By now you know your objective and why you want to attain it. You've also intensively researched your subject.

This step will identify the marketing targets that will make your empire richly rewarding — and why they would buy.

So far you've been concerned with your own needs, what you want to share with others, why you want to dedicate time and energy to that sharing, and what you must know to have something of substance to offer. A lot of "you's."

But unless you are paying yourself to read and hear your own words, it's now time to direct your focus to the source of empire-sustaining income: others!

In Step Nine, then, you must determine who those others are. You must know who would pay to read what you write or hear what you speak. Who cares that much, and why.

Nobody pays just because you want to share. They pay because they get rewards from paying. Benefits. In our empire-building world they pay for information and the benefits that information can bring them. They don't pay because you have a wish or a dream. They pay for the substance from that dream that meets their needs.

The shape and size of your empire is largely determined by the kind of information you disseminate, the breadth of your activities, the scope and effectiveness of the dissemination means used, the type and number of needs you meet, and the time and diligence you put into the empire's development and growth.

Step Nine focusses on the benefits, and, from them, how you find the most likely beneficiaries.

Let's make our point in a different way. If your empire is to generate income, that money must either come from others or you must print it yourself. If it's to come from others (the wiser of these choices), those paying must also get something in return. An artisan carves a statue. You buy that statue. You pay for the benefit of owning that work of art. A doctor treats your ailment; you pay for the benefit of feeling better or being cured. But if the statue falls apart or your health deteriorates, you will seek another artisan or doctor.

The point is obvious: if you expect to build an empire from selling an idea or information, or from a product or service related to that idea or information, you'd better figure out who would benefit from what you offer and why!

The process is as simple as our examples are plain: two lists from the research just completed, each in response to "Who would benefit by this objective?" and "How would they benefit?"

From the answers to the second question you can usually deduce when, why, and roughly how much they might pay, the "they" being the beneficiaries identified in the answer to question one.

EXAMPLE

Since you are explaining to others how they would benefit from self-publishing, you must already have a good idea what those reasons are. Yet, like the research just conducted about the topic, it is necessary for you, as an empire-builder, as opposed to a surface dabbler, to go beyond the fast and obvious reasons and create comprehensive lists of who would benefit and why.

Much of your information comes from the research just completed. But you might also ask both those who self-publish and still others who teach self-publishing the same who/why questions, to draw even more information from their knowledge and experience.

In the first list, "who would benefit from knowing why and how to self-publish?", ten categories come from that research and those questions:

1. authors/writers
2. idea disseminators
3. specialists
4. businessfolk
5. entrepreneurs
6. teachers of communications and related fields
7. speakers
8. academics
9. those involved in the process: typesetters, designers, printers, etc.
10. people in general

Naturally there is some overlap from one category to the other; better that than deleting a category altogether.

As to why or how they would benefit, self-publishing could provide:

1. better control of the appearance and content of the end product
2. better control of the marketing and distribution
3. greater product development by their empire
4. more profits
5. greater tax advantages
6. faster product development
7. greater prestige, by being in print
8. material in print that reinforces oral presentations
9. material in print for classroom use

"Peeling an egg does not put it in your mouth"

Jewish folk saying

"No classic resembles any previous classic, so do not be discouraged."

Ernest Hemingway, 1956

Thoughts and suggestions...

Successful Seminars

What do many successful seminars have in common? They follow this guideline:

Sell hard-to-find but easy-to-apply information to participants who perceive that it will meet their needs.

The key words are *information* and *perception*.

The information must be something that the listener needs to know but can't easily find, won't find, or prefers to pay to hear about. It must then be presented so the listener can begin to put the information to use the moment the talk ends.

Perception is more important. Not only must a potential seminar registrant feel the need that the seminar would help solve, the solution must be apparent.

For example, everybody lauds a seminar that helps raise low self-esteem — even those with low self-esteem. But unless it's clear in the title and description that those with low self-esteem should be there, unless they immediately recognize themselves and their needs, and unless they feel that the seminar will help them, that seminar will either be given to a small gathering of the wrong people, for the wrong reasons, or the hall will be empty.

Source: *Speaking For Money*

10

Other Kinds of Research

"Heavens," you say, "get on with it! All these lists, all this time wasted while somebody else steals my idea!

"What more can there be? I've finished my research. I know the benefits, beneficiaries, resources, needs, and goals. I've got a handle on my core subject. I know how the information can be disseminated. What else could possibly keep me from launching my empire right now?"

Nothing. Launch away.

Of course, you might be like the man who wrote the geography book after he saw his first city.

So Step Ten suggests six ways to explore your subject more fully before you flail away. Each is limited in scope, but the six combined should take you to almost all of the hamlets, fjords, and backwaters that need and response can create. How much better your geography book will be!

Granted, it's easy enough to take a subject, any subject, and divine some ways to develop it. You might even strike the golden lode with the first blow of your exploratory pick.

But if you're sincere about realizing your objective through an empire that grows to nurture you as it helps others, a less superficial exploration seems in order. Rather than striking the first ground in sight, a resolute look about would surely suggest more fruitful diggings.

What follows, then, are six ways by which you might address your core subject, each designed to match the variables — the topic, means, benefits and/or beneficiaries — differently. The purpose of Step Ten is to help you explore your core subject as fully as your mind, common sense, knowledge, and purpose will allow.

All of which presumes that from the widest exploration will come the greatest variety of choices, and wisely chosen, the strongest possible empire.

Thoughts and suggestions. . .

Being in Print

Something you wrote that appears in print is a fleck of immortality, infinitely easier to reproduce than you are when your earthly time is over. The words are proof that you creatively existed, a tangible something to be shared with and read by your great-grandchildrens' great-grandchildren. That is a dream every bit as worthy as filling your pockets with coins and your living days with recognition.

———————————————

There's hardly a literate soul who can't be in print. But there are millions who won't expend the simplest energy to learn the basics and try. What a shame. The rewards outweigh the cost a hundredfold.

Source: *How To Sell 75% of Your Freelance Writing*

10A

Sub-Topic Pad

When you conducted your initial research one of your pads was titled "sub-topics."

You might have divided that pad into the various means, then noted "potential articles" every time you saw a way that your subject could be approached differently for a different readership, or "potential speeches," "potential book," "potential audio cassettes" — including as many of the means as seemed appropriate or for which you saw ways for further development.

You might also have used the "sub-topic pad" as a doodle pad, where you noted the "what if..." thoughts that sprang from your means notations or from others' treatments of your core subject.

At this step separate that pad from your research material so you can more fully develop the ideas it contains.

This form of research-based mental exploration may be as reactive as original. For example, articles you read about the core subject may suggest facets that aren't mentioned, or are underdeveloped, or could be developed far more. A how-to piece might suggest a matching article of case studies showing the how-to guidelines in action. An article might suggest a series, or a state-of-the-art update, or a perspective piece setting the facts into a more intelligible base.

Whether you are reacting to another's treatment of your subject or the doodling stimulates new thoughts that could be developed by writing or speaking, the use of sub-topic notation during research can be the basis of and a spur to further thought now. It can also be further explored by the other techniques explained in the next five sections.

EXAMPLE

Perhaps the best way to share this as an example would be to take a peek at selected pages of your sub-topic pad, typeset here so that all can read your cacographic scrawl.

A word of explanation first: we know that these are first thoughts, not fully reasoned conclusions. Some are solid and could lead to beneficial advances if pursued, some might work if modified, and some are flights of fantasy, unintelligible (to us), or just plain dumb ideas. The reason for putting everything down on the sub-topic pad as it occurs is that nobody knows with certainty which idea is brilliant, bad, or bizarre when it's still in its rawest form. Or which of the plain dumb variety now could become the bulwark of brilliance later. Best to record them, to be reviewed every now and then, after plucking out and developing the seemingly best-at-the-time first.

From the "Potential Articles" section:

1. What kind of specialty people want to self-publish? Easy to get to them. Articles and ads in their own magazines, to sell the book.
2. Focus on very rich/very successful. They'll want to tell others how they did it. Most can probably write: articulation is needed for success and writing. But the successful are used to getting others to do sweat work. So an article for them would tell how they can write a book, control its appearance/distribution, make $$ from it — but how they can get a ghost to do the writing/bk production.
3. College profs want to be in print, have class-related materials they have to get reproduced anyway. They could self-publish their material, sell it through the bookstore. Check it out: restrictions by bookstore? Or would their college/university insist on printing it, making the profit? If feasible, see which classes use the most paperwork of the repeat kind. Find the magazines those teachers read, write very simple how-to articles explaining self-publishing process, with costs/profits. Stress profits/captive audience.

4. "How To Self-Publish Your Family History" — would need to check good guides for family history. Family/seniors magazine. Need to get some of family to commit to buying it before had it printed. Could be run on computer too.

From the "Potential Book" section:

1. Two points here: books about self-publishing and books people can self-publish.
2. Check and see how many easy-to-follow, current, solid self-publishing books are out. See what each covers: copy/compare tables of contents. What sections are poorly covered? Which need annual update? Which need good examples — more, better, wider variety — than these books contain? Think of filling those needs.
3. What kind of specialty books likely to be self-published aren't covered directly, well, or specifically by books in (2)? Workbooks? Exercise books? Elementary school materials? Corporate in-house: ledgers, invention diaries, new idea booklets?
4. A how-to book on self-published promotion items?
5. Tie self-publishing into local books: directories, travel brochures, etc.
6. Do a book showing how to self-publish using laser-jet technology, plus other info about marketing.
7. Is the info sold by computer self-published? How does a report, for example, sold by modem differ, other than not being printed by me, then bound? Is this a self-publishing field still unreported? A book? Sold by modem or printed and bound?

From the "What If. . .?" section:

To show how one idea might appear more than once on your sub-topic pad, as a follow-up to an earlier idea or in the respective sections according to the primary means of idea dissemination (articles, books, tapes, etc.), let's select three insertions from your "What If. . .?" section that are directly related to (2), (3), and (4) of the "Potential Articles" section, appropriately numbered, in the same order, (2), (3), and (4) here.

2. The hardest thing for a rich/successful mogul to do, if he/she wants to self-publish a book but farm out the hard part (editing/book production), is to find a qualified person to do that well. What if my empire included just that service? Three ways: (a) me, (b) me and direct staff, (c) me and minimal staff and reliable writers/book developers, on percentage. Might hook into a distributor and fulfillment arrangement with finished books. Would require consulting at earliest stages; could tie that into other forms of writing, such as articles about person, book, etc.
3. Profs/teachers can read and follow instructions but timorous about innovation/expenditures. Could include in article or author bio the address to receive a free instruction sheet (or "10 Steps..."), and then send flyer with good freebie explaining full, step-by-step, action-and-cost case study (or 2/3) that we could sell to respondent. That could lead to any other services, seminars, tapes, booklets that we might offer that would be appropriate.
4. The same idea for family history. What if we provided a detailed, how-to explanation/case study showing format, means of assembly, kinds of binding — the essentials — for a solid book that could be bought/given to family members. Might go further: show how to organize the family around this book. Tie together taping the oldest members, photographing and album-combing for earliest pictures, cartography, early record checks, date confirmations — the key steps of assembling the history, then the inexpensive but lasting means of preserving the material.
5. Why can't this be done — (4) above — for corporations that focus strongly on history, internal development, skunk works, legends around the founders and doers? We could either provide the framework — how to gather — or we could gather/produce the book?

10B

Grid

A second way of exploring information is through the use of a grid. Two lists are required. One will be written vertically, with horizontal lines extended to the right after each item. The second will be written horizontally, with vertical lines extended downward after each item.

For illustrative purposes let's say that the first list consists of five letters, the second, five numbers. Thus our grid will look like this:

	1	2	3	4	5
A					
B					
C					
D					
E					

What kind of lists might you use in your grid? Perhaps the benefits that others (or you) would receive by the realization of your objective, the beneficiaries, the means, or the sub-divisions of your core subject. And many more.

Taking our example a step further, let's say that the vertical list is of the five most likely means of idea dissemination by which you would share your information: articles, books, seminars, tapes, and consulting. And the horizontal list is of the five most likely beneficiaries: welders, doctors, elves, lawyers, and oboeists. Thus our new grid would look like this:

	welders	doctors	elves	lawyers	oboeists
articles					
books					
seminars					
tapes					
consulting					

So much for the grid design. What do you do with the boxes you've now created?

You ask a qualifying question, then put the answers in the boxes. For example, "By which markets would these beneficiaries most likely be informed about my subject?"

Or you simply juxtapose two lists and put anything in the boxes that comes to mind, as a way of seeing new relationships between different variables or as a prod to provoke different qualifying questions.

The latter is self-explanatory.

But the use of a "qualifying question" begs explanation. The question in this case might be that just asked. You may have a question in mind first, then find or create the lists of the needed variables, or you may just have two lists of variables, then formulate the questions that those lists might answer.

The answers go in the boxes. In the articles/welders box you might list trade magazines in the welding, plumbing, manufacturing, energy, maintenance, or machinery and metal fields. You might list specific magazines, you might put them in priority order of likely article acceptance, you might note whether they pay on acceptance or publication, what they pay, etc. What you put in the box is your decision and will likely be affected by how much detail you want or need and by which facts are available.

To follow the example a bit further, under books you might list the firms that publish information about your topic. For seminars, the kinds or names of sponsors that you might seek for programs to those beneficiaries. For tapes, who produces similar tapes or by which avenues you might make tapes available to the beneficiaries. Consulting? Through whom, or to which groups, might you consult.

If you can't think of anything to put in a box? The box about consulting elves might be a good example. Leave it blank. Ideas don't always occur simply because you have space to fill. Nor will all lists harmonize well. The purpose of gridding is to identify the obvious relationships and expand upon them to the degree that your imagination, the facts, and your research allow, as well as to discover the new relationships that otherwise might go unnoticed had two dissimilar variables not been pitted together.

Is it worth all the hassle? Who knows until you try? The obvious ways to develop your subject will be just that — obvious. And your empire might flourish with distinction though you never poke below the skin. But there may also be five or fifty ways more to develop an idea that could be the difference between acceptability and roaring success — or just one revolutionary, million-dollar, people-saving way that nobody ever thought about because they never bothered to rub two simple items together to see what breaks out.

Why not try it? It does take time and it makes you think. So do empires. You thought they came instantly, pre-thought and pre-built?

EXAMPLE

Before one self-publishes a book it is necessary to determine who will buy that book. From there, why they would buy it and how they would use it. And finally, the best form the book should take to enhance that use and encourage that purchase.

An important element of the form of any book is its binding.

So both to test the process of gridding and to think through various kinds of books in terms of the kinds of binding, you juxtapose two lists — of assorted kinds of books and the principal kinds of binding — and you ask a question of each mating, "How appropriate is this binding for this kind of book?"

Your grid would appear as follows, though instead of boxes (because of space limitations) you use letter/number identifiers, which are explained after the grid and a brief definition of the forms of binding.

FORMS OF BINDING: KIND OF BOOKS:	perfect	staple	spiral	cloth
popular/bookstore	A1	B1	C1	D1
textbook/bs.& lib.	A2	B2	C2	D2
cookbook	A3	B3	C3	D3
trade/mail order	A4	B4	C4	D4
workbook/car repair	A5	B5	C5	D5

A few words of explanation about the forms of binding might be helpful.

Perfect binding is the kind used by most trade paperbacks containing more than about 60 pages. The cover is actually wrapped around the bundled and roughened page ends, then glued, but the reader sees a continual, squared-off cover over the spine that usually includes the book title, author's name, and the publisher's logo. This flat spine is ideal for library identification when the books are vertically stacked.

Staple here refers to some form of wire stitching, either where the staple is on the fold ("saddle stitched") or where it is driven through from the front to back cover ("side stitched") The first is limited to very short, or thin, items (about 80 pages maximum); the second can be used for several hundred pages. In either case, the book or booklet has no spine.

Spiral can be a continual spiral wire binding, like that of a stenographer's notebook, or a heavier plastic comb, often found on large business manuals. These are impossible to identify when stacked vertically, often get tangled when shipped or handled, and the pages can be pulled out easily.

Cloth refers to the many forms of binding of hardback books. These resemble perfect binding, with a spine printed or stamped to identify the book. Some cloth books are also covered by dust jackets, which are printed paper protectors with graphics similar to paperback covers.

Your purpose is to ask how appropriate each form of binding is to each kind of book, to eliminate those that are totally inappropriate, to identify (if possible) the "best" form of binding, and to see what additional thoughts your focus on binding might suggest about other elements of the book.

Here is your analysis of each of the 20 possibilities:

Popular book for bookstore sale:

A1 (perfect): preferred form for paperbacks, with spine for vertical display, easy handling.

B1 (staple): may be mandatory if book is too short, will lower price, must be displayed face out.

C1 (spiral): acceptable if book must be laid open when used, as workbook or cookbook, but must be displayed face out. Plastic comb increases bulk, difficulty in handling/stacking, raises price.

D1 (cloth): fine, all benefits of perfect bind unless dustcover required.

Textbook for bookstore or library sale:

A2(perfect): best form for bookstore; library will probably prefer the cloth edition. Both ideal for stacking, if clearly identified on spine.

B2(staple): must be displayed face out in bookstore, taking up too much space for lower-priced item; can't be identified on library stacks so will likely be kept in vertical files or not purchased.

C2(spiral): some textbooks must be used open, such as lab instruction books or typing books, so spiral binding is necessary and bookstores selling texts will carry it; libraries seldom buy spiral bound items because they have no spine and damage more easily.

D2(cloth): fine for bookstores since hardbacks bring a higher profit and, because textbooks are often mandatory, that helps reduce the return/loss ratio. Libraries prefer cloth, if the title is clearly identified on the spine.

Cookbook:

A3(perfect): difficult to keep a perfect bound book open when the user's hands are mixing and cooking — book won't lie flat unless held down on both sides.

B3(staple): same problem, unless the book is very short and the pages can be folded back, which damages the book for long-term use.

C3(spiral): usually the best form; most sought by buyers planning to actively use cookbooks.

D3(cloth): same problems as perfect bound. If it's really a display or gift book, to be left on the table and browsed through rather than used in the kitchen, cloth will justify higher price.

Trade book to be sold by mail order:

A4(perfect): two considerations are its photoability, for use in advertising and promotion, and its mailability. Perfect binding mails well.

B4(staple): same as above.

C4(spiral): wire spiral must be specially wrapped or it will cut through conventional mailing wrappers; plastic comb is heavy to mail and may cut through.

D4(cloth): same as for perfect binding, except that it will be heavier to mail.

Workbook about car repair:

A5(perfect): like the cookbook, if it is to lie flat while being used, perfect bound isn't preferred.

B5(staple): also hard to use flat.

C5(spiral): best if to be used as a manual.

D5(cloth): if the book is to be an encyclopedia or reference, cloth binding gives the best long-term protection, but will not lie flat if the book is to be used, open, for actual repairs.

Some grids are comparisons betwen two lists of variables to see what ideas are inspired by their interaction. Your grid is the listing of factual information you might have culled from Dan Poynter's *The Self-Publishing Manual*, a leisurely browsing in a library and downtown bookstore, the replies to questions asked the acquisitions librarian and the bookstore manager, plus some common sense.

Of what value is your grid?

1. It increases your knowledge about binding, for your own use and to share with others.
2. It provides basic information about which you could become more expert, to prepare an article, book, speech, or seminar.
3. It could be expanded to form a chapter in a larger book about self-publishing — or publishing in general.
4. It could be expanded, with illustrations, into a handout to be circulated to other self-publishers, to validate your expertise, to attract potential clients for your mailing list, to get your name before others, to share valuable information they need to know, etc.
5. It could be adapted into a talk, with visuals, to help actual or potential self-publishers, and in the process help establish your presence and display your expertise.
6. It could provide valuable background insight needed for the development of a new form of binding that improves upon one or many of the existing forms.

7. It could be the topic of a detailed booklet describing everything any self-publishing hopeful, beginner, or practitioner would need to know about binding, with how-to steps, flow charts, schedules, providers, costs, case studies, etc. One booklet or one of a series that describes fully the entire self-publishing process, in short components for easier segment updating.

8. It could be used a dozen more ways that a dozen more needs dictate. Having the information in grid form provides a malleable source of usable data, easily reformed or expanded, to fit into needs yet to be seen.

This grid was devised to answer a question, "How appropriate is this binding for this kind of book?"

But once the facts are in place, incomplete as they are, one can ask a series of new questions that come from the new knowledge and from simply thinking about the subject:

1. What is the best form of binding for "x" kind of book, in terms of (a) cost, (b) durability, (c) salability, (d) convenience of use by the buyer, (e) weight, (f) mailability, (g) appearance, (h) profitability? For each kind of book, which values are critical? Can the values be listed in an order that will apply consistently to all books of that kind?

2. Is it possible to develop a binding that allows the text to be laid flat and still has an attractive spine large enough for clear identifiability?

3. Can a comprehensive and reliable description be developed of the kind of books that should use each form of binding?

4. Is it possible for self-publishers to bind their own books in the best way with today's binding tools? Could those tools be changed so that self-binding would be affordable?

5. Is it possible that many books in the future will be prepared directly from computer print-outs, and that a binding technique could be devised now for that future need?

6. Or that books in the future will contain both paper and protectable inserts, perhaps containers for disks or electronic program tools, and that the current needs will have to be modified for those demands? Could a binding be devised now to anticipate, or be ready for, that need?

To answer some of these questions you would need new grids, more information on your current grid, or even a crystal ball.

Grids provide information, bring together facts, facilitate insights, provoke new questions, and expand your thought process into the "what if?" realm. The kind of questions that be troublesome. They force you to build from the known; they provide sensible paths and surprise glimpses into the unknown. They push you to the basics, the corners, the edges, and the core of your subject. That provides substance and depth to an empire.

"Others go to bed with their mistresses; I with my ideas."

Jose Marti, 1890

"Every author should weigh his work and ask, 'Will humanity gain any benefit from it?'"

Nachman of Bratslav (1770-1811)

Thoughts and suggestions. . .

Keeping a Seminar Afloat

There are 14 basic elements to a seminar: subject, feasibility study, description, title, market identity, sponsorship, presentation, handouts, product sales, booking, price, time, location, and promotion.

Of the 14, three are crucial for proper launching: subject, title, and promotion. If any of these fails, the ship sinks. The rest are more forgiving. Unless they are grossly distorted, they can be brought into line once the vessel clears port.

Source: *How To Set Up and Market Your Own Seminar*

10C

Working and Secondary Questions

Earlier, in Step Six, you formulated a working question from your purpose statement. Now you must use that question as both a tool of exploration and organization.

The question defines your quest, so further definition of the question, through the use of secondary questions, will refine even further what you want to know and do.

Let me say that another way. Your purpose is stated in one sentence. By converting that sentence, or statement, into a question, then moving toward answering that question through asking (and answering) of secondary, related questions, the process propels you in ascending velocity toward the answer of the working question.

For example, if your purpose is to teach literacy to all middle-aged immigrants, your working question might well be, "How can I teach literacy to all middle-aged immigrants?"

By answering how that can be done, you take a giant step toward doing it. You also eliminate thousands of ways it can not or should not be done.

But you can get still closer to the answer by asking secondary questions. Those almost always begin with the journalist's best friends: who, what, why, where, when, and how.

For example, the working and related secondary questions in this case might be:

"How can I teach literacy to all middle-aged immigrants?"

1. Precisely whom would I teach? Those who can't read? Write? Or both? Would I teach them to read and/or write in English or in their native tongue? And what is "middle-aged" in this context?
2. What level of literacy do I want the middle-aged immigrants to reach?
3. Why do I want to eliminate illiteracy? Do I want to teach them something else while making them literate?
4. Where do I want to teach them? In one locale? Nationwide? Worldwide?
5. By when do I want to eliminate this illiteracy?

By asking the working question, then the secondary questions, you zero in on your precise goal and, by extension, you reduce the ways and highlight the means involved in bringing the purpose to reality.

If, for example, the purpose is to teach illiterate immigrants 40-55 years of age living in Ojai, California sufficient English to vote, read instructions, and be able to function adequately with public services, and you wish to do this at the local high school within a two-year period, that is far different from wanting to help all immigrants in the United States from 35-60 reach full fluency, in their own language or English, within the next 20 years.

The method used to teach literacy may be the same in both cases, but almost everything else will be far different. Locating the illiterate in Ojai might take a week or two. It would be much more complex — a staggering task -- nationwide. A classroom might suffice in Ojai, where television might be the necessary mode of instruction across the land. You get the idea. The working question sets up the topic and points the direction; the secondary questions help delineate the boundaries and means.

The answers to the working and secondary questions are, of course, useful in themselves. But they can help even more.

Imagine that you are going to write an article or book or deliver a speech or seminar about your subject. The same starter words used in secondary questioning are those used in developing an outline or table of contents for each of these, and virtually all other, forms of idea dissemination. As well, the same questions and answers, usually reassembled in a similar pattern, often appear for all of the means of idea dissemination about the same topic.

The outline or table of contents puts the working and secondary questions into a logical, or at least intelligible, order. The process of identifying those secondary questions, putting them in order, and creating an outline or table of contents becomes one more way to develop your core subject. It forces you to see your subject in a different way. And seeing your subject in as many ways as possible is what we are about here.

EXAMPLE

Self-publishing is your core subject.

Your purpose statement is: "I want to show people why and how to self-publish."

Thus "Why should and how can people self-publish?" is your working question.

Finally, to derive secondary questions that will help you better define how you can achieve your purpose you will use the five "w's" and the "h" of journalism: who, what, why, where, when, and how.

The process differs only slightly here because of the complexity of your double-verbed working question. The result is twice as many questions, or more!

1. Who should self-publish? Why?
2. Who can self-publish? Who can't? Why?
3. What kinds of materials should be self-published? Why?
4. What can be self-published? What can't? Why?
5. Is location a factor in self-publishing? How?
6. What is favored for self-publishing by location? What isn't? Why?
7. When should one self-publish? Why?
8. When can one self-publish? When can't it be done? Why?
9. Specifically, how should one self-publish? Why should it be done that way?
10. Who cannot self-publish that way? Why? Are there other ways those people can self-publish? What are they?

These questions did not slavishly follow the key words. Rather, "why?" was asked at virtually every step, since in this case it is in response to that question that the "how's" of self-publishing are most easily understood.

There are more questions to be asked beyond those that adhere so closely to definition, such as:

11. How does self-publishing differ from other forms of publishing?
12. How much does it cost to self-publish? What profits can one expect from self-publishing? How do the costs and profits differ from other forms of publishing?
13. How does the role of the publisher differ, in terms of time involvement and the skill need, between self-publishing and other forms of publishing?

Plus many more questions, limited largely by your breadth of interest and interrogatory vision and curiosity, that could cast new light on the subject of self-publishing.

Most think of self-publishing in terms of books, but the term and concept would be as valid for other forms of idea dissemination, such as articles, audio cassettes, video cassettes, and films. In each case the questions above directly apply, as well as additional questions specific to the respective means.

Why bother to turn questions into questions? To define and to reveal. Then, from a clearer understanding of what additional information you need to know, to formulate the answer(s) to your working question, which often assume(s) the organizational structure of an outline or table of contents.

A working question and secondary questions are the very heart of orderly research. Answers are easy. Asking the right questions, then taking those answers to continue to ask the right questions, that's the kind of no-nonsense probing that leads to successful empires.

"Nothing accomplishes nothing."

Bahya Ibn Puquda (1050-1120)

10D

Asking Around. . .

This technique hasn't a very dignified name and it can assume as many nuances as you have investigative skills, but it can also strike closer quicker to imperial pay dirt than any other. Just by asking around. . .

And the line separating it from your earlier research, involving interviews and first-hand information gathering, is also imprecise. It may be a matter of degree and intensity.

On the surface, "asking around" seems simple enough: you ask what you and others want or need to know about your core topic. But two things complicate the process: asking and listening!

Few are good listeners. Most are pleased that they have asked an articulate question and are thinking of how they will repeat that marvelous feat. If they hear, and comprehend, the words in reply, it is to pluck one as a launching pad for their next query. They are more concerned about pace, flow, and not losing face.

That inattention can be caused by what they asked and how they asked it. Stock questions like "How are you?" and "What's up?" are usually salutations not expected to reap literal and profuse replies. Other questions are part of the game of positioning, with the complexity of the question or the display of "in" words used to show what the questioner already knows as much as to solicit a desired response.

So some of the skill of good listening comes from asking questions that evoke replies that you want or need to hear. And asking them so the respondent will reply fully and without reservation.

That reservation often comes from an unstated question, "Why do you want to know?" The respondent has no point of reference for the question so he doesn't know how to frame the answer — or whether it wouldn't be more prudent just to keep quiet. Suspicion and distrust can turn full and open responses to monosyllabic grunts — or silence.

Several guidelines might help:

1. Study your working and secondary questions.
2. Also determine what others not knowledgable about your core subject want or need to know about it, so your empire can help provide that additional information, plus any services that its provision would create or require.
3. Separate the needed information into two categories: that which is best acquired through impersonal research and that best obtained through first-hand, direct replies or the personal sharing of observations and opinions.
4. Research those items that don't lend themselves to personal interrogation.
5. Determine who might have the knowledge or experience to respond to the remaining items.
6. Establish an honest reason for wanting to know the information.
7. Then ask those knowledgable people most able or willing to give full and understandable replies, recording the responses and sources as you·would any research findings, as described earlier.

Reducing the process to guidelines makes it seem unduly stiff and formal. The art is to make it casual and enjoyable, which comes from practice. Once mastered, there can be boundless opportunities in planned and general conversation to further expand your knowledge, if you practice attentive listening and purposeful asking.

Best yet, artful "asking around" will continue to prove valuable once your empire is established, as a means of seeing if you are on track, what new information is available to share, and where new needs are still to be met.

EXAMPLE

Let's say that you see one point that is of utmost importance to every self-publisher and you think that by being thoroughly knowledgable about it your expertise and presence would easily spread to other facets of the field.

The point? The time and cost factor of converting copy into camera-ready pages.

"Desktop publishing" are popular buzz words related to that point. To computer buffs they mean one thing, to the impecunious newcomer facing an aging typewriter and eager to pound out the first page of a manuscript they mean another. If you could position yourself between the two, to provide the hard facts and current information, convert "WYSIWYG" talk into hours and dollars, provide intelligible state-of-the-art advice related to the many needs of self-publishing, you'd be selling tickets to the fastest turnpike. You'd be sought, needed, and — soon, you hope — rich.

So you study the issue and decide that there are two ways to establish that pivotal expertise, each necessary for the fullest benefits: (1) case studies and (2) contemporary how-to advice, plus projections for the near/far future. The first — reliable facts about the watch versus the checkbook — requires hard research; the second, "asking around."

The problem: how do you get the data and others' talking time without creating suspicion or mumbling resistance? If they think you're out to build an empire on their time, or take advantage of their information-sharing, either could be the result.

One way is to convert their information and time into an asset for them. So you tell four self-publishers that you are going to write an article about their latest self-publishing project, each chosen because it used a different technique. The article will compare the time/cost effectiveness of each approach. A much needed case study! You explain clearly what you need to make the results understandable to their peers, what you will do to make the data provision easy (provide fill-in charts, call for the information, let them call the data to you by modem collect, etc.), and you offer to keep their name and their firm's confidential, if they wish. You explain to each participant how this information will help others, plus how many copies of the article you will send them, with a letter (plaque, certificate, etc.) of gratitude. You determine what has value to each person and try to provide at least some of it for their cooperation.

The advice, state-of-the-art, and future projection information is best suited to blatant "asking about." You find some of the information in print, deduce some of the rest, but most of your time is spent talking with those in the know, those with their thumbs on the pulse of change.

Why would they talk to you? Because (1) people like to talk, (2) some simply know more than others and aren't reticent to share it, (3) some want others to know that they know more than others and are glad to share it, (4) some like to help and will share if they think the listener(s) will benefit from the exchange, and (5) some benefit from sharing. Most fall into several categories.

You decide that a good way to tap all five categories is to gather information for an article and later a book. That way, unless what is said is given with specific and stated restrictions, all that you hear can be used again and widely. Facts are public domain; their wise use and strategic spread can be the bulwark of your empire.

Since purpose statements and working questions are the soundest starting blocks for all forms of idea dissemination, you formulate purpose and working questions for your article(s) and book, just as you did for your empire.

You want to position yourself so you must be read or consulted by self-publishers in need. To do that, your purpose will be to provide the most accurate, understandable, and fully usable information about converting their copy, quickest and most economically, into camera-ready pages. Thus your working question might be, "How can the self-publisher convert their copy into camera-ready pages quickest and most economically?"

Your case study already shows, in dollars and hours, what has worked best with other self-publishers. But because it focussed on actions passed, your articles (and book) must include the changes in techniques, technology, costs, and quality.

Where can that information best be found? Among members of trade or professional groups or associations, in their newsletters, on the magazines and bulletins the members read, in their bull sessions, and by flat-out asking around among those gathered or others they suggest or mention. So you join, mix, ask, note, ask another, read, ask, and always (then or later) get the facts on paper or tape.

You also seek out the product vendors, particularly those on the cutting edge of innovation. In this case, the hardware and software computer developers creating and selling the myriad of new items related to desktop publishing. The danger comes from aligning yourself too closely with one product or process, unless it is clearly superior. And then for too long. So you find out everything you can about anything new or different that ties desktop products to self-publishing.

Finally, you write your article, and another, and likely a third — then the book.

That's how you position yourself as the most knowledgable and reliable self-publishing information source about desktop publishing from among the many hawkers and gawkers in the field. By writing and speaking. By putting your case study results and your recommendations about current practices and purchases, and future directions, in print, clearly and with conclusions and guides for immediate action, where they will be read and acted upon.

You submit your articles to the newsletters distributed to members of self-publishing clubs, groups, and associations. You write your articles for magazines that appeal to self-publishers, writers, entrepreneurs, and other information merchants. You rewrite your articles for business and industry magazines that publish in-house, adjusting the angle of your piece so its conclusions apply to those readers' needs.

And you speak to the same groups, and others, focussing on the new desktop publishing phenomenon, about the revolutionary concept, now a reality, of putting publishing in the hands of the literate masses, about what that specifically means to the listeners you are addressing, and how — one, two, three, four — they can make it work for themselves.

What you are selling is information. You can get most of it by simply asking around. What you ask and how you use what you hear depends upon what you want to do with it and why.

Since you want to show yourself as an articulate, knowledgable source of current facts and future directions, you need the information and you need to display your articulation, by writing and/or by speaking.

Asking around doesn't replace research — it is a means of research. But it goes farther than the formal structure that term implies, because as long as you have a tongue, good ears, an inquisitive mind, and a companion (or many) who know something that you and others would benefit from knowing, the technique is readily available to use to expand your expertise.

So you do use it, then you process what you hear wisely. Your article leads to another, and then to a book, then consulting and speeches and tapes.

It's said that the best writers are the best readers and the best speakers are the best listeners. Empire-builders need to read *and* listen avidly and with a purpose. Then ask the kinds of questions that produce empire-building answers.

Thoughts and suggestions . . .

Selling Your Writing

Amateurs write, then try to sell.

Professionals sell, then write.

The tool that makes the difference? *The query letter*. A one- or two-page letter that sells the idea and, through its writing and contents, convinces the editor that its writer should also prepare the article.

When the editor replies positively, the professional crafts an article to meet the interests, needs, and desires of the readers and that editor, who is their buyer.

Chances of a sale? Far better than 50% for a query-approved submission. Maybe 5% if sent cold, without the query.

The difference is even greater in time than it is in percentage. So great, in fact, that unless the amateur starts marketing like a professional fairly early in the game, and writes to match, he or she will likely never get there.

Source: *Query Letters/Cover Letters: How They Help Sell Your Writing*

10E

Topic-Spoking

A nother way to provoke new thought about your core subject is to extract, then focus on one aspect of it — say, a word, use, benefit, beneficiary, or means — to see what that aspect brings to mind in terms of realizing your purpose.

You could form a mental imprint of that aspect, then say or write down what that image suggests. You could say it to others and hear their responses. Or, if you want to record the process and responses for later use, you could write down that aspect and all of the related words and thoughts it stimulates.

There is a way to record that information, with an uncomplicated diagram, so it can be used again and again to expand your subject's exploration. Put the starter word(s) expressing that aspect of your subject in the center and those that are suggested by it in a circular position around it, linked to the center by "spokes," like a bicycle wheel. Let's call that "topic-spoking."

Instead of "aspect," let's call the word(s) in the center of your diagram the "core topic." The spokes would be the lines emanating from the core topic outward, and each thought suggested by the core topic, resting on the end of a spoke, a "point."

Graphically, it would look like this:

point ——————— **core** ——————— **point**
              spoke   **spoke**

Let's create a complete example of a topic-spoking diagram by using the word "writing" (or, for greater precision, "idea dissemination by writing") as the core topic, then ask ourselves by which means of writing could we disseminate ideas?

The writing means that come quickly to mind are articles, books, signs, newsletters, press releases, scripts, ads, and fillers. There could be as many spokes as there are means, although we limit the maximum in this book to eight because of space and graphic restraints.

Adding in the eight spokes and points, our diagram would look this way:

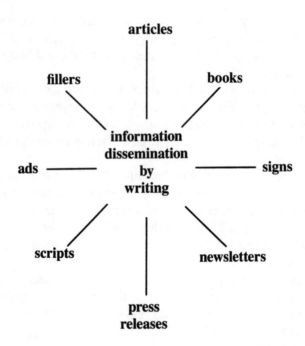

Since our empire will be developed by speaking as well as writing, let's create another diagram around "information dissemination by speaking," identical in form and purpose to that for writing. Again, the first means that come to mind are talks/speeches, seminars/workshops, radio, training sessions, audio cassettes, video cassettes, television, and consulting, which would be graphically expressed as:

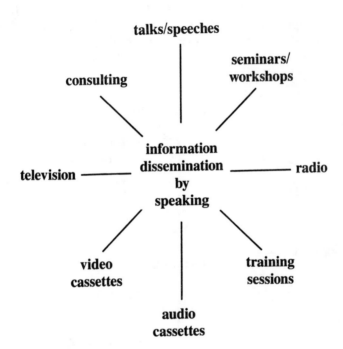

What do the diagrams tell us? That these are means by which we can disseminate information, one by writing, another by speaking. But what if you want to disseminate a particular kind of information? What if your mission is to warn junior high school students about the danger of drugs?

Two obvious advantages to the written or permanently recorded topic-spoking diagram are that (1) it can be used again and again without rethinking the process or spokes, and (2) the spokes and the points are totally flexible: they can be removed or replaced at will.

Therefore, you can change the core topic and try the original diagram, retaining what works, deleting what doesn't, and adding in new points for new means or word associations. Or you can create completely new diagrams.

Let's try this with our second diagram, "information dissemination by speaking," here changing the core topic to "drug information dissemination to junior high students by speaking" — simplifying it on this example, for lack of space, to "drug information by speaking."

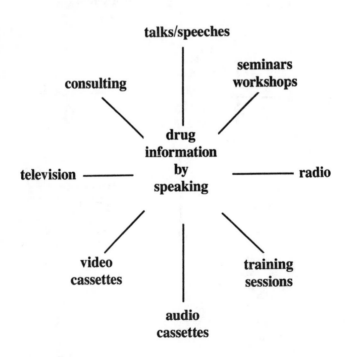

After changing the core topic, you ask yourself, which of these means would work for this new audience about this subject? You pluck out those that wouldn't work at all and add other speaking means that aren't here but, for young teen listeners, should be. And if you wish to list them in order of importance, noon-high for the most important then clockwise in descending order, you would probably also change the order from the previous core topic.

What if you were interested in seeing how videos might serve your purpose? How could you most effectively warn junior high schoolers of the dangers of drugs through the use of videos? The points would, naturally, depend upon the core topic, so how you phrase that will help guide the kind and depth of idea exploration that results.

Let's say that you were interested in knowing what form of video would be most effective at the junior high level. More specifically, what kind of person should narrate or be the main character in this video. Your points then would be the kinds of presenter such a speaking means might need. Perhaps your diagram would look like this:

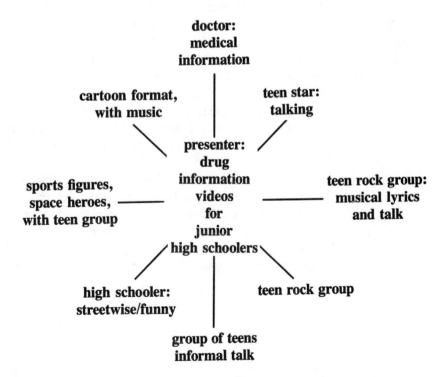

There are as many diagrams as you have questions, ideas, topics, and means, all clustered around the same larger goal: to realize your mission.

What is the value of topic-spoking?

If you limited yourself solely to your original core subject, you would be but one deep in each means of information dissemination: one article, one seminar, one speech, and so on.

But by further defining your subject and creating secondary questions and core topics, you extraordinarily expand your scope. Subjects one deep are paths to penury, while subjects with dozens, scores, or hundreds of offshoots are the things from which empires are built and bountiful lives are led.

As important, much of the information you have already gathered from other research, by gridding, and from developing the working question can both be directly applied to this process and can be significantly expanded.

In addition to greatly increasing your knowledge and potential income, topic-spoking can significantly reduce your research time for the volume it yields. Finally, it can provide you with a visual tool that will make later vertical development of your subject easier to see and quicker to do.

Must it be done in the spoked form? No, but by separating the many topics in this or a similar fashion yet tying them back to the core subject, it should help you separate and see topics easier, thus facilitate their comparison, reduce repetition, help identify interrelatedness, and — later — link them vertically, for better marketing.

Mind you, topic-spoking isn't the same as laying the physical bricks of empire-building. Contemplating who will narrate a video isn't the same as hiring the narrator or selling the tape. Spoking is more akin to making rough sketches for the blueprint.

But don't kid yourself that rough sketching is just game-playing, though it is easier to erase the errant line than to insert a brick under a sagging building. Alas, it's for exactly that reason — to place every brick where it should be in the first place, the right number in the right row — that the doodling and spoking and gridding and working questions are asked now, moved about, erased, and every variable is explored and explored and explored.

EXAMPLE

You want to share information about self-publishing with others. Moreover, you want to build a livelihood with an exciting and profitable future from that topic, and by so doing also gain the rewards of sharing expertise. Thus you need to approach your core topic from as many angles as possible, counting on the combined income from many means to bring you the desired fame and fortune.

Your first step would be to see which of the means of information dissemination might lend themselves to explaining self-publishing, as we have already done, in a rather preliminary way, in the two diagrams above. Then you must topic-spoke each of those means to find angles or approaches by which you can profitably disseminate information about self-publishing through them.

Let's look at four of your topic-spokings:

Articles

Start by writing the word "articles," then your core subject in the center of the circle. Then you ask yourself, "What articles could I write about self-publishing that potential doers need to read?"

Notice the word "need." That separates the idle page flippers from those who will purposely seek out that particular issue on those specific pages; it is the difference between an article an editor might use and one that he or she would eagerly buy. Empires thrive on eager buyers, not possible users.

So you focus on what readers need to know to put the information to use. In other words, articles with strong "how-to" angles. Expository pieces full of practical, nuts-and-bolts contents. Examples are crucial here: facts, names, costs, results, sources.

Since you concentrate on what readers need to know and thus will buy a publication to read, your chances of selling to the editors of those publications they would buy is excellent — far better than 50%. Later it will be up to you to package this material and sell it like a professional, almost always through a query letter, then provide, in final form, a manuscript about the same topic and as solid as the query promises.

But for now, before picking your readers and their editors, how would your topic-spoking appear for such articles? One version might be:

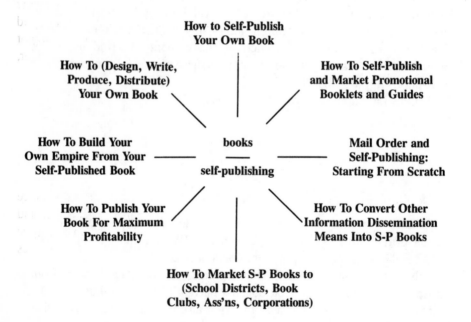

Thinking in terms of titles when it comes to articles explains why this topic-spoking reads as it does. Others think of topics *per se*, so, for them, some segments of the above might read: "self-publishing greeting cards," "self-publishing poetry," or "the finances of self-publishing," which corresponds to "Why Accept 10% of the List When You Can Earn 100% of the Profit?"

Where have you drawn your eight spokes from? The kinds of things others might self-publish (books, poetry, company manuals, and greeting cards), examples of people who self-published successfully, the financial wisdom of self-publishing, what self-publishing can lead to (an information empire), and the switch story (when *not* to do it). Frankly, you could have 20 spokes here, and as you developed those, another 20 topics would emerge.

And where did the knowledge to topic-spoke the articles come from? From the initial research you did about the topic, other items in print, and from what you want to know more about in the field. Plus a giant scoop of common sense wrapped around universal greed: what's in it for the doer, and what must that person do to get the honey?

Books

Topic-spoking books about self-publishing isn't vastly different, since most articles can be beefed up, buttered with examples, indexed and bibliographied, and made into books. That is, most article topics can be stretched into books, alone or bonded with other articles. What book titles have you hung on your spokes?

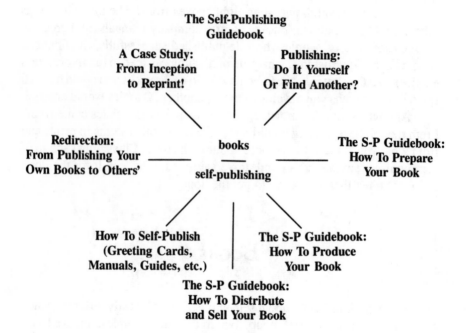

Reading clockwise from the top, the main self-publishing book, a how-to like Poynter's or Ross's, is the most likely book about the subject and surely the best to establish your expertise most widely — if it's good!

Then, whether one should self-publish or not, followed by three sub-books, which you could pull from the main book as separate excerpts or you could fatten up with more depth and examples. These could be published as the boxes indicate — in fact, there could be at least six boxes, each a step of the process of total self-publication — or you could combine them into larger books.

More than books can be self-published so the spoke pointing to 7:30 suggests three, of a dozen, kinds of books you could write that would explain how the respective products could be produced following a similar process.

For people already self-publishing their own materials but thinking of joining the mainstream of commercial publishers: a book telling how it's best done! And a case study showing rather than telling, that carries a book from the idea to the second printing.

You could literally write 15 different books from the eight spokes shown, plus another ten, perhaps, from ideas that will emerge as you continue to research the subject.

Seminars

Will people pay to hear you talk about self-publishing? At the speech level, where the time allotment usually runs from 15-60 minutes, the subject is too complex to give more than the most general or perfunctory presentation. Fine for a quick, spirited display of expertise but too little time to really impart much lasting information.

But for seminars, with from three to eight hours of direct explanation and exchange, the subject would work well. Many want to hear such an explanation so they can ask questions and relate it, verbally if necessary, to their own situation. Then they want written directions, which allows you to also sell your books or related products to the most interested participants.

What kind of seminars might you offer? Again, by title, these might attract sufficient numbers to make the time, travel, and workbook costs worthwhile:

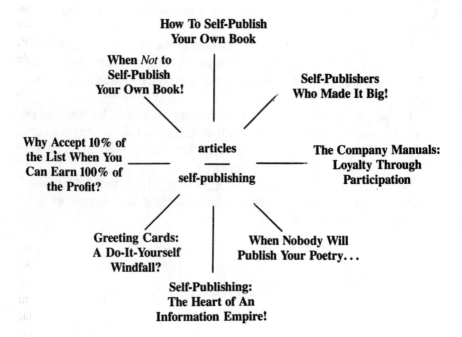

You ask yourself what others would pay to hear. More important, what benefits would be sufficiently attractive — or what needs sufficiently frustrating if not met — to convince them to set aside part or all of a day, drive a distance, find parking and the room, endure hard seats and immobility, and pay for all of that? The answer seldom varies: money (meaning profits) or immortality (meaning the creation of something that will validate the participant's existence now and may endure to be appreciated by their grandchildren's grandchildren).

Self-published books usually meet both criteria. Seminar titles, however, must be fairly explicit about the profits or immortality. At least they must be sufficiently attractive to overcome others' natural inertia and suspicion.

"How To Self-Publish Your Book" is contextually similar to the article or book by the same title, but packaged differently and reinforced, in this case, with a workbook that gives examples of what is being said. A similar seminar discussing promotional booklets and guides (as examples of the dozen or so other items one can profitably self-publish), as well as one that discusses each of the steps of the process (which could then be three, five, eight different seminars), again shows how you could turn eight profitable spikes into 18.

Self-published books are usually sold by mail, thus by combining both processes, "Mail Order and Self-Publishing," you expand the attractiveness of the offering.

Experienced information disseminators will see self-publishing as an ideal way to produce items to sell through other means so you sugget two seminars directed to that market: one that shows how they can convert their speeches, seminars, articles, tapes, and other information dissemination items into self-published books; another showing how the larger process, through self-publishing, can lead to an empire.

It's not enough just to mention profits to some. They want to know precisely how much profit — and how to double that! The result: a seminar.

And the biggest frustration in self-publishing: selling the damn books! So as many seminars can be well launched as there are solid, different markets for book sales. Each market can be a separate seminar, similar groups can be combined, or all the markets can be linked into one presentation.

Video Tapes

Would anybody buy video tapes about self-publishing when they could get most of the same information in a book or at a seminar? Topic-spoke it and see!

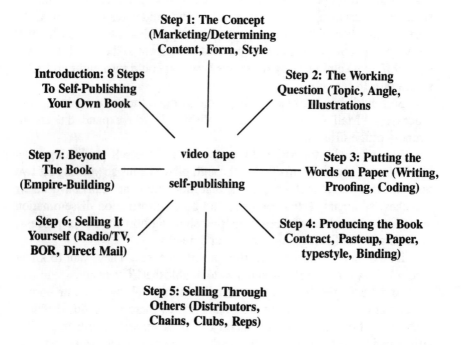

Step 1: The Concept
(Marketing/Determining
Content, Form, Style

Introduction: 8 Steps
To Self-Publishing
Your Own Book

Step 2: The Working
Question (Topic, Angle,
Illustrations

Step 7: Beyond
The Book
(Empire-Building)

video tape

self-publishing

Step 3: Putting the
Words on Paper (Writing,
Proofing, Coding)

Step 6: Selling It
Yourself (Radio/TV,
BOR, Direct Mail)

Step 4: Producing the Book
Contract, Pasteup, Paper,
typestyle, Binding)

Step 5: Selling Through
Others (Distributors,
Chains, Clubs, Reps)

They might indeed if the buyer had to pay many thousands of dollars to produce a first-class self-published book, a video tape series (perhaps with a workbook) clearly showed the steps that must be taken, and the same video series cost far less than the risk of producing a book that fails.

Particularly if each video tape replaced the need to attend a seminar to see and hear the instructions being shared — or if that material was only available on that tape.

The eight-step series topic-spoked above is one way that videos could be effectively used. Each tape might also focus exclusively and in high visual detail on such specifics as paper selection, type choices, cover preparation, page layout, binding, the choice and placement of illustrations, and so on. . .

Topic-spoking. A simple diagram that spreads all of the ideas around a common core. It works if you do.

It works even better if you play with it more. The next chapter shows how.

"Of the making of books, there is no end."

Ecclesiastes, 12

"If a man look sharply and attentively, he shall see fortune; for though she be blind, yet she is not invisible.

Sir Francis Bacon (1561-1626)

"Many are stubborn in pursuit of the path they have chosen, few in pursuit of the good."

Friedrich Wilhelm Nietzsche (1844-1900)

Thoughts and suggestions. . .

Professional Speaking

"These are the basic steps to success in professional speaking: (1) have something to market; (2) get all the "tools" you can to be able to share with the world who you are, what you are, and how you can help the client's group; (3) market yourself, and (4) keep working on getting better and better."

"How do you break in and rise to the top? By having something to say -- and then honing that message, your delivery skills, and its marketing through constant attention and repeated practice."

Source: *Speaking For Money*

10F

More Topic-Spoking

There are many more ways to use topic-spoking.

Point Prioritization

Let's expand on one use of topic-spoking that was mentioned in the last chapter, that of putting the points in some order. If your core topic was "markets for speeches showing how to create loyalty to a product," and, say, eight good markets came to mind, they would be the eight points at the end of your spokes.

You might want to list the best market at the top, the next best at about the 1:30 position (using a clock face for descriptive purposes here), the next best at 3 o'clock, and so on. Then, to indicate how you have put the points in order, you might change your core topic to "best markets for speeches showing how to create loyalty to a product, in order," or start that mouthful "prioritized best markets for. . ."

Why bother? One, this forces you to investigate the points to establish that order. Two, it gives you a rough market list that shows where the greatest percentage of booking time and energy should be directed. Three, it gives you a diagram that could be used for other speeches or in other ways.

In the last case,.you might use the same diagram but change "loyalty to a product" with "loyalty to a company." Would that be another speech for the same markets? Would that be a speech at all? Or would just some of those companies be interested, and from them you could create a new circle of points, with new markets and a new prioritization?

Remember, topic-spoking is both a practical tool and a way to move information and conjecture around to create new ways to see your subject. We are doing both here.

Bunching Points

Sometimes the points run the full gamut, none similar. But at other times the points will be similar, related, or part of a progression, and you may wish to move them near each other, if for no other reason than clarity. In the case just cited you might have as potential markets four car manufacturers, three in the cosmetics retailing field, and another producing hamster food. By bunching the like markets you might strike upon other ideas common to them, and have the similar markets at least gathered together in one place.

A stronger example might be where the points were the steps of a process. Your core topic might be "how could we create a market for hamster food?" The points might suggest eight key steps to creating a product and a demand. If four discussed the product and four the demand, by bunching the like groups together, you can see two distinct areas where seminars, training sessions (of people, not hamsters), video development, and promotional tools might be directed.

Nothing ingenious here. Put like points next to each other. Then, if you wish, prioritize them.

Imagination in Core Topic Use

Clever core topic use can make all of these mental machinations well worth their cost in time and paper.

That is, the demand you make of the diagram will generally determine the value of the ideas and mental associations you get from its points.

Some of the core topics are obvious, yield valuable information, and must be done.

In the previous chapter the examples asked "by which means could the subject best be developed (or presented)?" For empires based on writing and speaking, the means are critical core topics. In fact, should you wish a more precise vocabulary for this methodology, you might call all topic-spoking that uses the means as the core subject "means-spoking."

In an earlier exercise you listed the benefits that one might receive from your realizing your goal, and who would receive those benefits — the beneficiaries. So those too are obvious core topics, and could result in "benefit-spoking" and "beneficiary-spoking."

We have just discussed potential markets for a speech, so "market-spoking" would be a welcome addition to your supply of knowledge, though it overlaps much with "beneficiary-spoking."

But don't stop there. If you are asking as a core topic, "How can I best share my recipe for soy souffle?" or have simply put "soy souffle recipe" in the center of the circle to see what mentally gathers around, let your mind wander and your core topics proliferate.

"How can I best share my soy souffle recipe — in food magazines?"

"How can I best share my soy souffle recipe — in Europe?"

"How can I best share my soy souffle recipe — as the core of a training diet for runners, swimmers, cyclists. . .?"

"How can I best share my soy souffle recipe — in Japanese?"

"How can I best share my soy souffle recipe — on television, to promote my book on soy cooking?"

Making Core Topics of Points

The ways by which you can wisely use your core topic will be dictated by your imagination and the limitations of the subject. One way to find new core topics is to complete a topic-spoking diagram, then move each of the points to the center to try as core topics. Sometimes that changes the perspective so that a whole new universe of questions and information emerges that can be reslanted for different readers/listeners/beneficiaries or a new way appears by which information can be shared.

Let's look again at a diagram from the previous chapter. Remember, the full core topic was "drug information dissemination to junior high students by speaking":

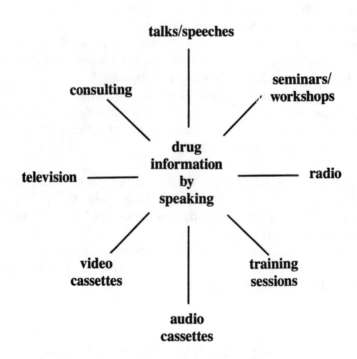

We actually did move video cassettes into the center in that chapter, but why not the others, one at a time, to see what results?

For example, let's move television into the core topic position, and leave the points at the end of the spokes simply as letters.

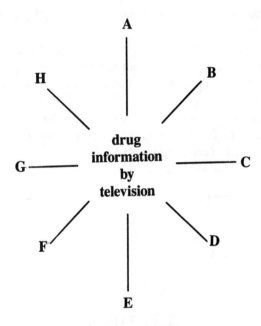

Keeping in mind that you are dealing with junior high schoolers, you have two courses of action. You can just leave the above as it is and replace the letters with any idea, thought, question, or word that comes to mind, placing them directly on the diagram or writing them on a list, to later try on the diagram those that have something in common.

Or you can ask a secondary question or tag on some qualifying words, to directly seek a specific kind of association for the lonely letters above.

You might add "formats" to the core topic, and replace the letters with various formats that might provide drug education to junior high schoolers, later, perhaps, putting them in some priority order.

You might add "personalities," then list the names of people whose speaking on TV would help impart needed information. You might add "kinds of personalities," then list the types, perhaps noting specific names under each type.

You might add, under television, "shows," if you think that your campaign would be most effective through the insertion of information in existing programs.

How might you use the resulting diagrams again? If you have created a "TV personalities" diagram, why not replace "television" with "radio"? Or "videos"? Or "junior high school assembly personalities"? Or "junior high school assembly types"?

Topic-spoking is a tool, a way to see and develop relationships. It vastly simplifies the linking process, reduces research time, and makes empires possible from seemingly small subjects.

EXAMPLE

You decide to use an earlier grid example, about bookbinding, and topic-spoke it to see if it would benefit from this additional manipulation of its structure and contents. Here, though, you expand the earlier grid approach to ask, "If I wrote a book about bookbinding, to whom could I sell it?"

Your resulting market list might be topic-spoked in this way:

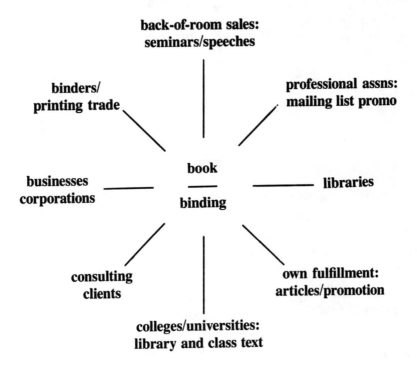

Thus, at each point (at the end of each spoke) you placed a likely purchaser, ranging from corporations to clients. Without any particular attention to the order.

Point Prioritization:

But if you wanted to use that diagram in a more precise way, you might ask, "Which markets are likely to buy the most copies of my bookbinding publication?"

That would require listing the eight markets in priority order, from that likely to buy the most copies to that likely to buy the least, based on research, guesstimates, and asking around to determine an order as close to reality as possible.

Your new prioritization might result in this diagram:

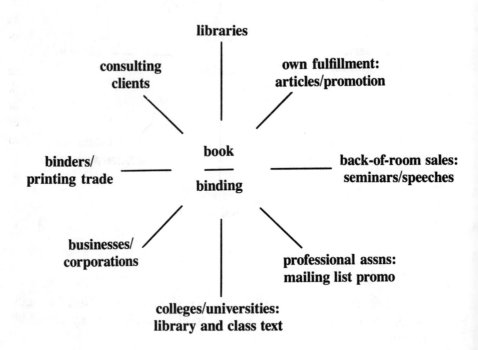

Then you test the diagram to see if the same order would prevail for related questions, such as:

1. Which markets will bring the greatest net profit from the sale of my book?
2. By which order will these markets purchase the book?
3. Which are likely to buy the most copies of the clothbound edition? Which of the paperback?

You then alter the order and points and you change the variables to correspond to the new relationship created by the response to each new question. It's simply easier and faster to begin from a pre-thought position than to start over each time, so you make your changes on an existing topic-spoking diagram.

You might also test the same topic-spoking periphery and change the core subject to ask, "How many of those markets would purchase a book about cover and page design for book publishers?" Or "paper selection for book publishers?" And while you are at it, why not ask if the other diagrams in response to the questions above would hold for each of the two new books?

The purpose again? It's a practical tool and a method to move information and conjecture around to create new ways to see your subject.

Bunching Points:

Your example only slightly lends itself to bunching. You rearrange the diagram to move closer together those markets that share something in common, as follows:

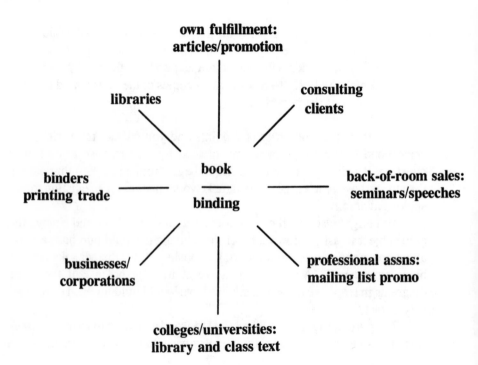

There is a tenuous link between the fulfillment and the consulting clients, in that both are directly tied back to you and your firm.

But there is also a loose connection between the first through fifth markets on the diagram. While clients are sometimes drawn through the fulfillment service, they are as likely to come from:

1. your seminars/speeches given at the professional associations and the colleges and universities
2. the products directly sold there, back of the room, and
3. mailings to those affiliated with these institutions

The other three are unrelated.

The value of this bunching? Not much here, except that by comparing this diagram with the earlier one that showed the order of the markets by likelihood of book purchase, you see that fulfillment (second in likelihood of purchase) is loosely related to four other markets.

That suggests that if you could make your listeners at presentations more aware of your fulfillment service, should they not wish to buy back of the room, and you could do the same to your consulting clients, you might be better able to increase sales from an already potentially good market. That sets you to thinking of better means of tying back-of-the-room sales to fulfillment follow-up, such as an attractive "later order form" or a later mailing directed specifically at those who buy back-of-the-room or for whom you consult.

Imagination in Core Topic Use:

You can realign your topic-spoking two more ways in search of additional information, relationships, and insights by "benefit-spoking" and "beneficiary-spoking."

But "market-spoking" is no innovation — that's what you've been doing this entire chapter — and "means-spoking" is precluded by the fact that of the many means only books need binding of the kind you are addressing.

In "benefit-spoking" the idea is to ask what benefits one would receive by, in this case, buying or reading your book about bookbinding. Those benefits are listed at the points. Your response to that challenge:

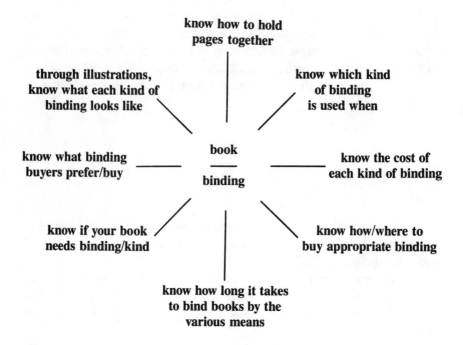

This diagram can be prioritized, one could bunch like benefits together — in short, all of the techniques used to expand knowledge can be applied, where applicable, to each of the parts of that knowledge.

You move from the benefits to the beneficiaries, asking who would benefit from owning or reading your book about bookbinding. Another diagram!

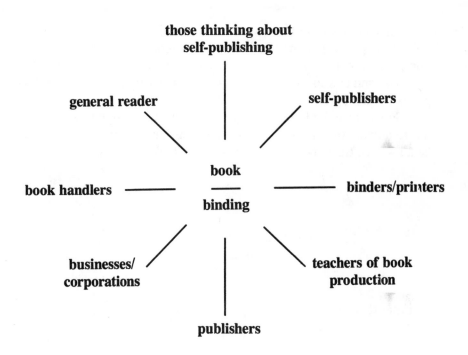

And another possibility to put a diagram in priority order or to bunch its similar points together.

The value of "benefit-spoking" and "beneficiary-spoking"? Both are of crucial importance if you decide to write about bookbinding, for they tell you who needs your book, what they expect to get out of it, to whom it should be directed (and, by extension, the previous knowledge they have, the vocabulary you should use, how they expect to use what you write, etc.) In short, the four elements suggested in this segment are very nearly those that will determine your success in virtually every facet of empire-building: what is the best means of sharing your idea or information, who will benefit, how, and who will buy what you produce or sell.

Making Core Topics of Points:

Another way to test new water is to take the points at the end of the spokes and put each in the center of a new diagram, then see what occurs. Sometimes nothing occurs. Sometimes a new perspective yields a bounty of insight and new angles to a subject. And sometimes something that the points suggest leads to a new, profitable path.

So you take the last diagram, about "beneficiary-spoking," and try this technique, full of expectations but realistic enough to know that it may be all wasted time and effort. That diagram looked like this:

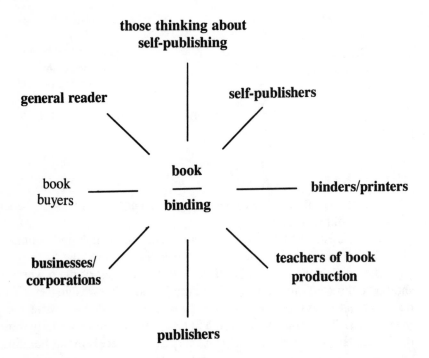

You decide to test the tool by moving businesses/corporations into the center, above book about bookbinding, and see what comes to mind:

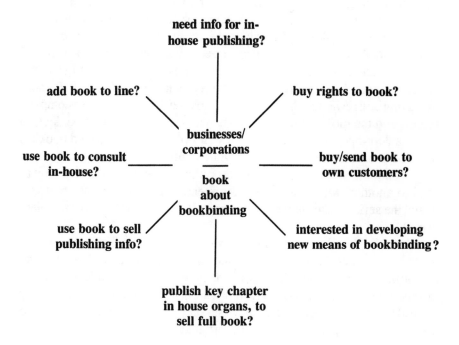

What occurs are eight avenues that the dedicated bookbinder, eager to empire-build from rather common knowledge learned to an uncommon degree, might pursue to gain a firm footing in the business/corporate world.

No point is so glaringly spectacular that the rest fall from their spokes. But in each there is a grain of need and thus profit, key elements to empire-building success.

To sell your book you may have to tease with a rewritten chapter, well placed in the house organ, free, to pluck the purchase order from the one person whose career can be scuttled by having the corporate annual report fall apart in the stockholders' hands.

Which businesses are selling books about publishing, printing, graphics, bookbinding supplies, tools that could be used for bookbinding, publishing software, etc.? Would they buy the rights to your book? Or its contents to program for the computer? Or would they add it to their line?

If you suggest new needs in the book, or means of bookbinding yet to be developed, wouldn't it make sense to see who responds, then get actively involved? Or seek out firms or entrepreneurs for a joint venture?

What about using the book as bait to hook consulting contracts, or a retainer, about bookbinding or the wider field of publishing? Perhaps extracting and rewriting that part of the book that directly touches company reports and the most common in-house needs, releasing it as a booklet, to use as a door-opener? Or the first of a series of publishing-related booklets released at regular intervals and bought by subscription?

Would that booklet make a good promotion item for one company to send to another, with their name prominently displayed on the front? Or would the series make such a promo, eagerly sought by the lucky recipient firms?

You could find a dozen more avenues waiting to be profitably walked for a subject as odd and as far from the usual bottom line as bookbinding and businesses or corporations. Imagine how many more little-known but income-yielding cul-de-sacs and well-travelled thoroughfares with plenty of need and eager buyers await the possessor of an idea or information who takes the time to play with all of the variables!

"If a man has talent and cannot use it, he has failed. If he has talent and uses only half of it, he has partly failed. If he has a talent and learns somehow to use the whole of it, he has gloriously succeeded, and won a satisfaction and a triumph few men ever know."

Thomas Wolfe, *The Web and the Rock*, 1939

10G

Topic-Tiering

U p to now we have been discussing the use of a diagram on paper, with a core topic, spokes, and points. Topic-spoking as a one-dimensional tool.

Yet empires built from writing and speaking are multi-dimensional, with an idea percolating up, down, and through the layers of information dissemination, often changing form and intensity according to the way it is expressed through the various means.

So another use of topic-spoking might be to stack like diagrams (or even unlike diagrams, at the risk of utter confusion) around a common, vertical core topic, to see how the points might provoke new insights. Why not call this "topic-tiering"?

Graphically, this involves a series, two or more, of diagrams that share the same core topic but have a qualifier at each level. The core topic looks like a vertical tube equal in diameter at each level and as tall as the tiers require. From it, at each level, emanate spokes, with points at the end of each. Diagrams are flipped sideways and stacked along a central core, like this:

"Writers, if they are worthy of that jealous designation, do not write for other writers. They write to give reality to experience."

Archibald MacLeish, 1960

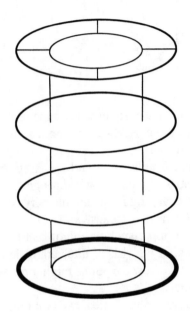

The qualifiers indicate how the tiers differ. Each tier may represent means, benefits, beneficiaries, products, markets, steps of a developmental process, etc. The idea is to see if a point, say, on tier one suggests a similar, identical, or related but different point on, say, tier four.

Which suggests at least two ways that topic-tiers might be created. One, take one topic-spoking diagram, make as many copies as you have tiers, layer them, assign each tier a different qualifier, and see which points work as they are, which must be somewhat modified, which must be changed altogether, and which must be eliminated.

And two, create one tier of spokes and points, then create each successive tier, using those of value from the created points and expanding, where possible, to add additional points.

What is the value of the multi-dimensional topic-tiering? It may help create a clearer mental image of the interrelatedness of the many facets of your subject that isn't evident in the one-dimensional topic-spoking.

By seeing an idea stacked by means, for example, it may become visually obvious that one article idea, a point on tier three, could easily be adapted into a seminar, on tier one, and from it could come a series of workbooks, tier two, and, later, a video instructional program (with the same workbooks, slightly rewritten) at tier four. How might this be represented? By a line drawn from one point at one tier to another point at another tier, with priority numbers at each level? By placing each of these islands at the three o'clock position so the linking is vertical? Use this tool as you wish. That's the beauty of tools of creation: you can create uses for them too!

Let's see how topic-tiering might work with our example.

EXAMPLE

To test this multi-dimensional tool you select "beneficiaries of self-publishing poetry" as the core topic that all levels or tiers share. To that you add "means" as your qualifier for each tier, specifically articles, books, seminars, and audio cassette tapes.

Therefore the structure of the topic-tiering looks like this:

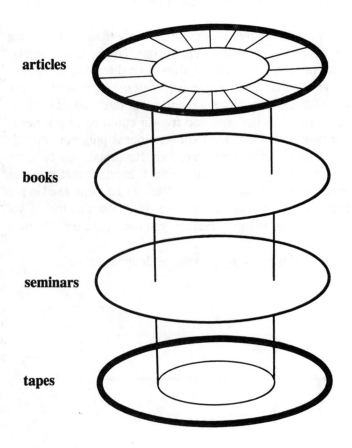

articles

books

seminars

tapes

Your first task is to identify those at each level who would benefit through that means from self-publishing poetry.

If your top level is articles and you begin at the top, you must first consider the core topic and the means. Articles and poetry are different forms of expression; one seldom self-publishes an article. So one would benefit from an article about self-publishing poetry. Like "How To Self-Publish Your Own Poetry."

The process of identifying such beneficiaries is straightforward. You ask, "Who would benefit by reading or writing that article?" And you write the replies as points at the end of your spokes.

Your points on tier one are (1) poets, (2) publishers of poetry books, (3) potential publishers of poetry books, (4) other publishers, (5) self-publishers, (6) printers, binders, distributors, and sales outlets producing or selling poetry books, (7) printers, binders, distributors, and sales outlets producing or selling small or short books, (8) potential publishers, printers, binders, distributors, and sales outlets of small or short books, (9) potential publishers of lyrics and/or musical scores, (10) entrepreneurs, and (11) the general public.

At the next tier, with books the qualifier, you ask "Who would benefit by reading or writing a book titled *How To Self-Publish Your Poetry*?" Not surprisingly, your replies place virtually the same beneficiaries at the end of the second tier spokes.

When you ask, at the seminar level, "who would benefit from offering or hearing a seminar about 'How To Self-Publish Your Own Poetry'?" and test each of the beneficiaries from the first two tiers, all remain as potential beneficiaries, plus others are added who are specifically linked to seminars.

Nor does it change much for audio cassettes.

That is to say that if one is benefitted by information disseminated by one means, if any other means provides basically the same information about the same core subject that same person would continue to be a prime benefactor.

One obvious advantage, then, is that in creating a diagram for one means, you have a starting diagram about that topic for any other means. You simply must test each point to see if it remains relevant for the second means.

Should you start, say, at the seminar level, you have a ready-made diagram to test at the book or tape or any other information dissemination level.

Some beneficiaries remain the same for all of the idea dissemination means, as long as the core topic doesn't change. But each means has additional beneficiaries.

For example, in focussing more tightly on articles, in addition to the 11 beneficiaries you have already identified, you find four more: (12) those interested in writing that article, who benefit by exercising and displaying their successful writing/marketing skills, (13) those writers who benefit by having their other achievements or their products mentioned in the author's biographical caption, (14) the editors/publishers who add to the value of their publications by having this information on its pages, and (15) those mentioned in the article itself.

You gain one multi-dimensional advantage, and save time, when you ask whether beneficiaries peculiar to one means, like those just cited, wouldn't also be benefitted by each of the other means. For example, as editors add value to their publication by having your article appear on its pages, book publishers get the same advantage by having your book in their line, seminar programmers benefit by having your seminar on their schedules, and tape producers likewise gain with more product variety by producing and selling your tape. Thus, by identifying an additional beneficiary at the article level, you have found another beneficiary at three more levels.

Another multi-dimensional advantage is that by being aware of similar beneficiaries at the various levels, it is easier to provide benefits to all of them. Those interested in self-publishing their own poetry, for example, will be extremely interested in an article, book, seminar, tape, or any other helpful means of information dissemination about that topic, and by your being aware of their existence you can inform them of the existence of products or services from the other means.

As well, you might be reluctant to write a book about this topic if you were only aware of those specifically seeking a book about self-publishing poetry. But your reluctance might properly fade if you realized the number of others wanting similar information by other means who would also be extremely interested in buying that information in book form. This multi-level awareness provides that insight.

Seen from a slightly different perspective, if you produce an audio cassette, or better a series of audio cassettes, about "How To Self-Publish Your Own Poetry," and mention them in an article, sell them at seminars, offer them for sale at talks, feature in a newsletter, refer to them in a book (or advertise them on the last page), and tell consulting clients about them, you are helping those interested in your topic by making them aware of useful information. By selling that information more broadly you are also strengthening your empire.

You focus even more tightly on audio cassettes and find eight more beneficiaries: (12) tape scriptwriters, (13) tape producers, (14) those interested in speaking on tape(s), (15) those who could benefit by having their achievements or products mentioned on your tape package or the possible accompanying workbook, (16) those mentioned on your tapes, (17) distributors and sales outlets handling tapes, (18) libraries buying tapes for their A-V holdings, and (19) those who sell items or services needed for tape production ·and sale, such as studios, duplicators, label printers, albums, etc.

Again, you take each of these eight to see if they, or their counterparts, might not be overlooked beneficiaries of the other means. Like seminar scriptwriters, seminar programmers, those who want to appear at seminars, and business or trade libraries seeking publishing items, and others.

By looking at the total diagram, all of the tiers as an interlocking unit, and considering the core subject and the qualifiers in the broadest sense, you may well find even more ways to share more information and expand your empire.

For example, rather than, or in addition to, producing a cassette or a series about "How To Self-Publish Your Own Poetry," why couldn't the poetry itself be taped and sold?

That's the kind of idea that adds an entirely new dimension to self-publishing, for publishing can be done by the stated as well as the printed word.

Could an article be written about "How To Tape Your Own Poetry For Profit"? What about seminars, talks, an insert for a newsletter, a new field for consulting, a book?

You produce a new beneficiary diagram at the tape level, identifying those who would benefit from taping poetry for profit. You then compare these beneficiaries with the four tiers already completed that were written self-publishing-oriented, to see if new beneficiaries can be found for either method, as well as to see what new ideas, like taping poetry for profit, occur.

Which is the beauty of topic-tiering. You can insert any diagram at any level to see if the new relationships stimulate new thoughts.

Topic-tiering, through cross-comparison of the points and qualifiers, as well as through the use of different diagrams to provoke new insights, provides a tool for idea expansion that is as rich as the core subject, the qualifier, and the mental creativity of the user.

For those intrigued by vertical integration of multi-media or multi-level variables, there are 50 ways — perhaps 150 or 1500 — by which topic-tiering can be made to yield new thoughts. It's a hacker's haven of the mind and paper for idea disseminators. For those with more linear tastes, enough has been said already in this chapter to march them to the bowels of bewilderment.

If topic-spoking works, and it does, topic-tiering simply uses topic-spoked diagrams that are turned sideways, then analyzed and compared vertically and horizontally. One can dabble with the probabilities forever, but if empire-building is the real goal, use it as long as it helps your empire grow.

"It's necessary to relax your muscles when you can. Relaxing your brain is fatal."

Stirling Moss, race car driver

"Nerve succeeds."

Jewish folk saying

PART
FOUR

Knowing Success

Thoughts and suggestions . . .

The Extra Benefit of Seminar-Giving

You never know when somebody listening to your seminar will turn your idea, phrase, or process into something entirely new that could change their life and the lives of all people.

More likely, by applying what you share many will be able to lift themselves from a drab, unchallenging existence to a more exciting and demanding plateau where they can better control their own destiny.

You must offer your seminar as if *every* person listening desperately needs to hear what you have to say. Then be patient.

Source: *How To Set Up and Market Your Own Seminar*

11

Action Paths and the Means

The purpose of Step 10, and its many parts, is to help you see your core subject as fully as possible. To identify and play with the variables, to match means with benefits and needs with beneficiaries, to mix the stew and see if the results are toxic or tasty.

In Step 11 you must draw conclusions from that world of "what if. . ." from which you can build an empire in this world of reality. Step 11 forces you to sort and pick hard values from dream numbers.

Now is the time to convert the insights you have gained into actual hands-on, practical ways to make your empire grow and yield.

To do that, you must determine the action paths necessary for the creation and fullest development of your empire, then stipulate the means of information dissemination by which those paths can best be followed.

EXAMPLE

You've looked at self-publishing from every reasonable angle and see four ways by which you could and want to share information about your subject that would be sought/needed by others and could be profitable to you: all requisites for empire-building.

One way is to tell others how to self-publish a book. Another is to show businesses or corporations how to produce and self-publish their own manuals. A third is to demonstrate how to integrate mail order and self-publishing, and a fourth, to explain and show how to self-publish one's own poetry.

By which writing and speaking means could you best impart the sought/needed information about each?

In the first case, you could tell others how to self-publish their own books through (a) articles, (b) a book, (3) college/university-sponsored seminars, (4) talks, (5) speeches, and (6) consulting. That would be your first action path.

Your second action path, showing corporations how to produce and self-publish their own manuals, might be composed of:

(a) in-house or self-sponsored seminars
(b) book
(c) video cassettes
(d) consulting

The third action path, showing how to integrate mail order and self-publishing, might be approached through:

(a) self-sponsored seminars
(b) college/university seminàrs
(c) association seminars

And your fourth action path, showing how to self-publish one's poetry, might be developed as follows:

(a) articles
(b) book
(c) college/university seminars
(d) talks
(e) consulting
(f) audio cassettes

How do you know which means are worth pursuing? "Means-spoking" and a couple of hard questions is a quick way to eliminate those that are clearly not. Questions like

1. "Has anybody ever successfully developed this or a similar topic by this means?"
2. "How successful were they?"
3. "If they weren't successful, how could I make it work for me?"

Plus other, even less scientific ways: asking around, common sense, and plain old hunches and guesses.

You are guessing at the appropriateness of the means at this stage. If in doubt, list it. Those which are inappropriate will be found wanting at Step 12!

Finally, you have no reason yet to prioritize the means. Later you will decide which action path (or paths) to pursue in which order. For now, pathfind, then means-match.

"Words should be weighed, not counted."

Jewish folk saying

"If you have an important point to make, don't try to be subtle or clever. Use a pile driver. Hit the point once. Then come back and hit it again. Then hit it a third time — a tremendous whack."

Sir Winston Churchill (1874-1965), on speechmaking

"Fill your mouth with marbles and make a speech. Every day, reduce the number of marbles in your mouth and make a speech. You will become an accredited public speaker — as soon as you have lost all your marbles."

Brooks Hays, 1960

Thoughts and suggestions . . .

The Beginner's Pitfall

Only beginners send in unsolicited manuscripts. Only beginners spend their time doing all of the research and all of the writing without having both a readership in mind and a positive reply to a query from an editor of a publication in hand. Only novices spend time before selling their words. That is the path to an unprintable future.

Source: *How To Sell 75% of Your Freelance Writing*

"Almost anybody can give a seminar. If you can speak, or even communicate in sign language, you can convey information to others, which is the essence of a seminar. The question is whether others will pay to hear what you have to say."

Source: *Speaking For Money*

12

Markets, Money, and Time

It's one thing to have action paths on paper, with the most appropriate means written beside them. It's another thing to convert those paths and means into reality.

It's one thing to know that the water is polluted, and a better thing to want to tell others how they can avoid the danger. But nothing happens until you do something with that knowledge and desire, until you effectively spread your information.

And that doesn't happen by itself. Converting knowledge and desire into action is neither magical nor instant.

To make action paths active and means of idea dissemination work, you must identify the right markets and use them in the best way.

Who are the right markets to warn about polluted water? Anybody who will be affected by that water or that pollutant! What is the best way to tell them? Shout it from every hill; print it in anything they read! No magic, just a pinch of common sense and some doing.

Step 12, then, is mostly a pinch of common sense — that rarest of commodities, always at hand and so easily overlooked — and another pinch to get you moving.

You've already identified the markets for your core subject: they are the beneficiaries, those most in need of what you want to share.

Remember, in this kind of empire-building your needs will best be met by helping others meet theirs. Your benefits will come from bringing benefits to those reading what you write and hearing what you say. They are your markets. How can you help them? By writing and speaking.

So if you know who would most benefit, what remains is to find out what those beneficiaries read and hear, then figure out how you can get your message to them through those means.

If that polluted water is in Lake Agua and it is located in the remotest corner of Idaho, *The New York Times* or *Izvestia* isn't the best way to warn that populace. Nor would a 30-second spot on a radio station in Tryon, North Carolina do much good.

The best way to reach that market is through a bullhorn on Main Street, signs all around the lake, a headline in the local paper, and fliers distributed at every door and left in every post office box.

And how do you get your message across? **POLLUTED WATER! STAY AWAY FROM LAKE AGUA!** Followed by simple, straightforward information about what would happen if the person drank it, swam in it, and so on. Common sense.

Common sense is the bulwark upon which empires are built.

Your task in Step 12 is to try to ferret out that common sense from a hundred other senses masquerading as simple, irrefutable wisdom and truth. Then figure out specifically how you will get the word before the eyes and ears of those most benefitted.

There's another factor too. Empire-builders need income and profits, and those are determined, in part, by the money their services will earn and the time those services will take. Thus money and time must also be noted with each market, so that all of the key variables are known by Step 13. That's when you will, at last, create a no-nonsense, prioritized, time-sequenced action plan!

EXAMPLE

In Step 11 you chose four action paths and selected the most appropriate means by which those paths might be pursued.

Presumably each, if successfully followed, would help you achieve your objective. Yet all paths and all means aren't equal. When you are hungry you eat rather than plant. When you are farming, planting comes first. And when you are empire-building, you must do both.

So now, in Step 12, you must investigate each of those paths and means, to see how to best sell your crop to the markets, what they will pay, and how long it will take to harvest.

This example will focus on one action path, three means, and three beneficiaries, though in truth you would subject each means of each path for each beneficiary to the same thorough scrutiny.

The Action Path

Here you focus on telling others how to self-publish a book, rather than the paths about manual preparation, mail order, and poetry.

And of the six means by which you will convey your information — articles, a book, seminars, talks, speeches, and consulting — you concentrate on articles, the book, and seminars.

Finally, you go back to Step 9 and review both the beneficiaries and the benefits they seek from self-publishing, and again you focus on three: specialists (in this case, in family history), speakers, and teachers.

The questions then become:

1. For *family history*/self-publishing articles, what are the best markets? For a book? For seminars? What do they pay? And how long could one reasonably expect to wait to receive the benefits: payment, prestige, spinoff?
2. For *speakers*/self-publishing — the same questions.
3. For *teachers*/self-publishing — ditto.

Answer that set of questions in the appropriately rewritten form for each action path, means, and key beneficiary and you have completed Step 12!

Family History

Articles:

The topic is "self-publishing a family history." The question is, who would even be interested in reading such an article?

Most likely those interested in history itself, in their family, in genealogy, and in the process of putting a book together and making it available to their kin. Who has the time and skills to seriously pursue the endeavor? Probably the older family members, with time and organizational skills and perhaps enough money to foot the expenses.

More guesswork. And common sense. But a good crosscheck is to see where such articles have been in print before, through the *Reader's Guide To Periodical Literature* or the academic indexes. They appeared on those pages because the readers were interested.

Next you ask what those most likely to read your article read. An excellent table of contents of magazines that buy articles from a wide range of fields is in the current *Writer's Market*. If you are seeking publications for the older reader, check "retirement," "general interest," "men's," or "women's." Look at the magazines listed under "history" and "in-flight." Check the index for magazine titles containing "family" or "genealogy."

Then you list the publications you think might run an article about your topic, noting the title, page number, pay range, length of response time to a query, and anything else of particular importance.

For example, you find a dozen likely publications in the "women's" section, others under "retirement," and still others elsewhere. Six of those are listed to show how all might appear on your worksheet:

Family Circle Magazine, 657 (1987), $250-2500, 6-8 weeks; how-to, for women.

Farm Woman, 657, $40-300, 1 mth; article appears year later, 1000 wds max.

Grandparenting!, 548, $75, 6 weeks; consider for reprint.

Modern Maturity, 549, to $2500, 1 mth; over-50 readership.

Ancestry Newsletter, 318, $50-100, 2 weeks; tight genealogy tie-in.

Parade, 300, $1000, 5 weeks; stress family project.

How long will it take for each of these to pay? In tender, as soon as the article is accepted, which could be several weeks to several months after you receive a positive reply to your query and submit the final manuscript.

But in prestige or spinoffs? Who knows? A piece in *Parade*, *Modern Maturity*, or *Family Circle*, particularly with a plug for related services or a product, could pay huge dividends quickly. Or there could be no apparent add-on value at all. It is up to you to parlay words in print into more words in print, through reprints and rewrites. And to use the fact that you appeared in a national or significant publication, or any publication, as validation of your expertise. Prestige and spinoffs from article use are by no means automatic, particularly if you are the only person who knows that item was published.

A Book:

Here the question is easier: since you are talking about self-publishing, is it important to you that your book be a model? That is, that it be self-published?

If so, you must first determine how you will get those eager to publish their own family history to buy your book, how much they will pay, roughly how many will buy your opus within a year or two, and whether you have the funds to pay for its production, promotion, and fulfillment.

Some working numbers? A 208-page book, with line drawings and halftones, sent by modem from your computer and set professionally, pasted by you, bid out for printing, cover done by a graphics specialist, 2000 paperbacks and 500 cloth 6" x 9" — $2.20 average. You sell it for $10.95 paper/$12.95 cloth.

Costs you $5,500 for the product, plus shipping and storage; $3,000 to market, maximum $10,000. Possible return, $28,375 — $28,000 after promo copies, damaged, lost, and relative's freebies (for you first book!). Profit, maximum $18,000, over 24-36 months.

In summary, then:

OWN BOOK, SELF-PUBLISHED: cost, $10,000; profit, $18,000; to prepare, 10 months; additional time factor: promotion, fulfillment. Equivalent to one solid year's work.

The alternative, though a bit shameful for one preaching self-publishing: have it published by another. Will still take as long in total to write, though the risk is far less. Draw up a market list of those houses publishing books about genealogy, history, how-to, self-publishing, and related topics. Put that list in priority order: most appropriate marketer, best pay, best advance, etc. Then query, with a full package, and only write when you have a solid, acceptable go-ahead.

Advantages: you just have to write the book; needn't tie up time or money in major promotion or fulfillment; publisher, hopefully, will market more extensively as part of larger line; pay will arrive regularly; once the book is out can concentrate on your next book.

Disadvantages: you give away about 90% of the income!

How, then, does the alternative compare?

OWN BOOK, PUBLISHED BY OTHER: cost, negligible; payment, 10% of list ($10.95/$12.95) paid every four months, with refund reserve held one pay cycle; 1-year to find publisher, 10 months to prepare. Will print 5,000 paper, 1,000 cloth; maximum profit, $6,770. Need $3,500 advance, will ask for $5,000.

Seminars:

Where does one find folks eager to exchange the comforts of home for a long-distance drive to a poorly-marked site to sit on a hard chair, be quiet, and pay for the privilege of hearing a seminar about how to self-publish a family history?

Almost anywhere, frankly. People are hungry for practical knowledge and a chance to do something that counts. Your problem is figuring out how to get them there and still make a profit well worth the many labors seminar-giving requires.

The first question: how much will they pay to hear you speak?

The answer: not much for this topic. Maybe $50 for four hours, with luck. They pay a lot to profit a lot. There's no profit on earth for publishers of family histories, or very little.

The second question: how easy is it to identify and inform those most likely to pay to attend?

The answer: very hard. Who, precisely, will beat the doors down to get the information in seminar form? Scattered seniors eager to share their memories and family trees with grandchildren just born? The rare soul who feels that those to come later deserve to know the triumphs and travails of their own family flesh? How do you put a flyer in their hands? What are their addresses?

So of the three major ways of financing seminars — through institutions, through businesses or associations, or by yourself — the third is out. Finding participants is too hard, so the promotion is too costly. And businesses/associations aren't interested in self-published family histories.

But colleges and universities encourage history and self-help, and their extended education programs regularly sponsor seminars with audiences just this ill-defined, counting on their mass catalog mailing to attract enough disparate people of like interests to pay the rent and the speaker.

The other possibility? Seminars to senior citizen groups or retirement clubs, for a set fee or by contract with a city or county agency.

How might this appear?

SEMINAR AT COLLEGE/UNIVERSITY: cost, negligible if driving distance near; profit, 50% of gross, approximately $400 plus back-of-the-room sales, $50-250; takes 6-12 months to get booking, offer program. Spinoff, consulting.

SEMINAR FOR SENIORS: cost, negligible if driving distance near; profit, $100-250 plus back-of-the-room sales, $50-150; booking hard to get, little spinoff.

Your back-of-the-room sales and spinoffs depend, of course, on what you have to offer beyond your spoken words. If you have your own book about the subject, that will bring the highest direct profit, though your own audio cassettes (singles or in series) can also be lucrative. Others' books and tapes can add to that income, and later consulting can both increase the booking's long-range worth and offer a further opportunity to help the participants put your message in action.

Speakers

Articles:

What do speakers read? Probably information related to their speaking topic and, when they can find it, information about speaking itself. So to put an article about self-publishing and speaking before their eyes, you would have to find both appropriate angles to that topic and the names of the publications upon which those eyes would set.

How could you broach self-publishing to a speaker? What would that person want to publish? And why would they want to do it themselves?

They'd most likely want to publish a book about something they knew and from which they would benefit by having their knowledge, so identified, in print. Again, probably the same topic, or one related, that they speak about.

They would self-publish it because (1) it would ultimately be far more profitable, (2) they could determine the book's appearance and contents, (2) it would be available quicker in the quantities they wished, (4) they would have all control over the book, particularly its marketing and distribution, (6) they would enjoy greater tax benefits, (7) no other publisher would publish the book, plus many more reasons.

Sometimes finding a title for an article, or even for the book itself, helps pinpoint the best markets. Some that come to mind from the information just gathered are

1. "How To Turn a Speech Into a Book!"
2. "From Tongue to Type: Putting Your Best Speech(es) in Print!"
3. "How To Double Your Income From Every Speech You Give!"
4. "Speak, Then Write, What You Know...."

The difficulty comes in finding specific publications eager to use such material. If the speaker is a C.P.A., for example, and that is what he or she speaks about, the specialty magazines for accountants aren't interested in articles about or directed to accountants who, God forbid, speak in public for pay! The titles above wouldn't be found on those pages.

(On the other hand, articles emanating from the C.P.A.'s speeches or the self-published book would presumably be prime material for accounting magazines. As important, such articles, if printed in the magazine on the condition that the bio tag line includes mention of the book or speaking, can be excellent promotional and selling tools for either, or both, as well as for the author/speaker!)

So the hunt for appropriate magazine markets is limited to the speaking field — and that, in print, consists of one commercial magazine, some academic offerings more interested in technical aspects of speaking (without pay), and two specialty newsletters.

The commercial outlet:

The Toastmaster, 225, several months, about $100; currently overstocked, seeks a Toastmaster tie-in.

And the newsletters:

Speakout (National Speakers Association), no payment, long delay in manuscript use; must be an N.S.A. member ($110/year).

Sharing Ideas! (for speakers), no payment, chops longer items into segments, sometimes serialized; must be a subscriber ($35).

In short, virtually no money can be made through self-publishing articles to speakers, but that could be offset by extensive exposure in *The Toastmaster* and specific exposure to the rather close-knit professional speaking world, or a sizeable portion of it, through the newsletters.

A Book:

The same question must be answered — will you self-publish it or let a publishing house produce and release it?

Even the profit ratio remains about the same as we saw for a family history book, roughly three times as potentially profitable by self-publishing as by having another publish it. That is little affected by a higher price, as books to speakers seem to charge. With good marketing, self-publishing pays. But the time involved may devour more than the profit earned, and there is always the risk that of 2,500 or 5,000 copies printed, all but 200 will sit in your garage until they or you qualify for Medicare.

Publishing a book specifically for speakers is a mixed blessing because it is so hard to find actual speakers. That's a bane when trying to place an article in a general magazine. But not so bad when you realize that professionals band together, and if you can infiltrate the gathering, in a positive sense, it is far easier to hawk wares to specialists through their inside channels than products to the general public.

Therefore, with a display ad, or several, in *The Toastmaster*; an ad or a flyer insert in *Sharing Ideas!*, and another flyer to the members of the National Speaker's Association, through the rental of the mailing list (you will have to become a member to rent the list), and you will have contacted many of those eager to buy speaking products. (There is additional information in the *Standard Rate and Data* publications about other rental lists for publishers' speech book sales, plus lists of seminar-givers.)

So should you self-publish your book to speakers, the time spent on promotion should be less because the scope of likely buyer contact outlets will be more limited and rather easily identifiable.

A final thought: to persuade speakers to buy your book specifically about self-publishing speeches or speaking-related material, you will have to convince them that you have something different and better to say than the other, more general "how to self-publish your own book" offerings both currently available and that you also contemplate writing!

For example, you may stress the point that your book will not only lead the speaker, step-by-step, through the self-publishing process, it will show how to plan the book's contents and design to increase its later back-of-the-room sale, as well as to serve as the first of a series of integrated products that will carry the book's theme into your market's working space.

Your book must include all of the self-publishing information the speaker can get elsewhere, hopefully clearer and more up-to-date. It must also contain additional material that directly addresses the speaker's needs, like specialty marketing, workbook and tape integration, other product linkage, and ten more things you must form fit to your reader's wishes.

Based on the above points, your self-publishing/speaker's book may well be 400 pages long, published only in cloth (hardback), and sell for $19.95. If you publish the book, you might note:

OWN BOOK, SELF-PUBLISHED: cost (for 2,500), $14,500; potential profit, $35,375; will take a hard year to write, produce, publish — needs specialty marketing later.

If you have it published by some other firm, they print 5,000 copies and sell them at $19.95, your worksheet notation might read:

OWN BOOK, PUBLISHED BY OTHER: cost, negligible; maximum profit (at 10% of list), $9,975; may take a year to find right publisher, nearly as long to write the book, but less risk in time until go-ahead given, advance in hand. Need $3,500 advance, will request $5,000.

Seminars:

An enigma here. Speakers will pay well for value received and there is a shortage of good, practical, applicable material around.

And speakers will agree that a book bearing their name will help establish their expertise, increase their earnings, and provide them with a source for articles, through which that expertise can be further spread and the earnings, though modest, increased.

The problem is finding enough speakers in one place to attend a seminar at which you can explain how to put the book together and use and promote it properly. And even if there are enough speakers in a general location, it's even hard getting them to attend.

Speakers generally lead other lives too. Few survive solely on their spoken words. So when the time is best for your seminar, it's also best for them to be booked or otherwise working elsewhere. Even if they aren't engaged, a final insult intrudes: they aren't very good listeners. Translated: this is a tough crowd to capture, and tougher to teach.

Seminars through colleges and universities that are directed at professional speakers? That's like trying to draw sinners to church through the Sunday Bulletin!

Two ways, if any, would work here:

SELF-SPONSORED SEMINAR: cost, $6000; potential income, from loss of $2500 to profit of $6000, plus back-of-room income of $1500-3000. Take six months to set up; spinoff, consulting and book preparation contracts from those who would rather let you prepare part rather than carry their book through every step.

The calculations are based on six full-day seminars, probably held in New York, Atlanta, Chicago, Phoenix, Los Angeles, and San Francisco. Average attendance, 20; cost $100 (lunch excluded). Costs: $1000, list rental, flyer prep, mailing; $900, two ads in *The Toastmaster*; $900, room rentals; $1300, air travel; $800, own costs; $600, program costs (workbook, coffee, etc.); $500, other.

The other method would · be to offer the program to the N.S.A. chapters, at the Winter Workshop, or at the annual convention held each summer. At the workshop and convention you must pay to attend to speak free, without a product sale! The chapters negotiate separately but expenses are usually paid and product sales are sometimes permitted. This would be done less to earn than to position yourself through sharing, for later (perhaps heavenly) reward or follow-up product sales and consulting. Your worksheet might say

N.S.A. SEMINAR (Convention or Winter Workshop): cost, registration fee (approx. $150-250) plus travel/room, workbook; profit, none; good for exposure, follow-up sales/consulting.

N.S.A. CHAPTER WORKSHOP: cost, travel/room, workbook; profit, free or modest stipend; usually will pay travel and some/all expenses; back-of-room sales, if permitted, can bring additional $300-1000. Excellent for exposure, follow-up sales/consulting.

Teachers

Articles:

Teachers are readers, so magazine articles should be right on target for such an audience. Yet the gist of your article ties self-publishing to the subject the teacher teaches, and that drastically reduces the number of receptive outlets.

Which is to say that very few magazine editors hear teachers begging for articles about self-publishing their own books.

Therefore, how strongly a magazine editor will feel the need to run such an article will depend, among other things, upon (1) how well you can convince that editor of the interest in and the need for your information by the magazine's readers, (2) how common self-publishing is in the field, and (3) the availability of good teaching texts and tools about that subject.

The personality of the teachers of that field is also important. Self-publishing is a risky and time-consuming business that requires speculative investment, production skills, and marketing. Many teachers are eliminated on one or many of those demands or skills.

So the trick is to find those specific fields where the concept is likely to be well received, then write a convincing query letter to the editor showing why your words should be on his/her pages. All the better if you can find others who have self-published in that field, wrap a how-to article around them and other successful examples, fill it with step-by-step information, and get the title of your book woven into the context or the author's bio, hopefully with the price and address so the reader can order many copies.

Which kinds of teaching fields are most appropriate for self-publishing? If you split the learning world (unfairly and quite arbitrarily) into academic and technical/vocational, the academic wing is far more likely to rely upon the established texts, with their occasional revision, while the technical/vocational group, though using textbooks and workbooks widely, will be more likely to want to write their own step-by-step and state-of-the-art materials, with frequent updates.

So if you want to publish an article to the academics, it would make more sense to tell them how to write textbooks and workbooks for the larger publishers. That is safe, acceptable to their peers, and profitable.

For the technical/vocational group, the same article, appropriately slanted, would be read. But so would the article you want to write: "How to Publish Your Own Textbook" or "...Workbook"!

Since these articles would appear in the teacher-directed magazines of the various fields, your pay would be meager to nothing. Therefore, as mentioned, you want to be certain that those readers who are interested in following up on your advice can find you or your products through the article or your bio tag.

Is there much hope of getting an editor of a high-paying general magazine to use an article telling teachers how to publish their own printed guides? Not really.

Some sample publication listings might appear on your worksheet this way:

Arts & Activities: 729, 8 weeks, $35-150; small, visual arts.

Computer Classroom Learning: 730, 2 mths, about $150; innovative ways
    to use computer in classroom.

School Shop: 734, 6 weeks, $25-150; industrial ed, high school and up.

A better source for such publications than the current *Writer's Market* is the respective indexes of the various academic disciplines, in the library.

Book:

The buying market for your book called *How To Publish Your Own Book About Nursing* (or Plumbing, Mathematics, Auto Repair, Writing, etc.) would be very small indeed. It's there — somebody always needs advice about how to publish a book about something — but the financial return on your investment in most cases would be ridiculously small.

Even the hottest new fields, like computers now, are apt to find the writers seeking established publishers or using more general texts, like Poynter's and Ross's about self-publishing, then figuring out the slight deviations as they apply the general process to their specific field.

You must make some hard calculations before skipping into the "self-publishing for ————————————— teachers" text. How many people teach in that field? How many need printed teaching tools? How many use texts and tools already in print? How many of those needing texts and tools are capable of producing them? How many of those want to? Of those, how many have the investment capital, time, skill, and perseverance to complete a book or workbook? And how many would follow it through the preparation, production, and marketing phases? While most of the responses will be rough guesses, the percentage of an already limited starting number finishing the last step will be extremely small. Then you must make your book known to them and they must buy it!

Alas, there may be a bright light in this narrow and unpromising area. Why not write a book telling how to market texts, books, workbooks, and teaching tools to special groups: technical/vocation teachers, liberal arts teachers, art teachers, teachers? Combine many fields into one and publish a book telling how anybody with, say, texts, tools, and products can meet the users' needs. That way those with a self-published item, plus all the standard publishers and productmakers, will need and buy your book. Leave the general information about book production to the general texts; focus on what can be done with that specialized book once it has seen print.

To make the book even more valuable (thus increasing its likelihood of being bought), give names, addresses, and phone numbers. Include facts, buying trends, needs not being met, future areas where books and products will be wanted, a current and annotated bibliography, a list of top magazines and newsletters in the field. Make the book a reference guide as well as a marketing tool, then update it every second or third year, inserting a mail-back, post-paid card in the book to be returned to be informed of the updates.

Based on this approach to one aspect of self-publishing, you decide to add to your worksheet information about *Computing and Electronics: How To Sell Your Own Books, Texts, Tools, and Products*. You doubt that a standard publisher will be interested, so you plan to publish at 208 pages, a trade paperback priced at $14.95. The book should cost about $2.10 apiece to print, with $3,000 budgeted for promotion and $600 for shipping and storage. You will print an initial run of 2000 copies.

OWN BOOK, SELF-PUBLISHED: cost, $7,800; potential maximum profit, $22,100; requires much additional research, which will take three months to complete, then additional nine months to write, produce, print book.

Seminars:

The issue here is the subject of the seminar, for teachers are conditioned to sit, pay (a bit) to acquire knowledge, and check college/university listings for new learning opportunities.

Programs would best be offered through the colleges and universities, or through the professional teaching and discipline-based organizations, at conferences, conventions, or as fund-raisers for those groups.

But what would the seminar be about?

An extended education program called "Teachers: How To Produce and Market Your Own Books, Workbooks, and Products" is certainly comprehensive enough to attract a wide audience. You may want to narrow that to cover just books and workbooks. The word "publish" is replaced by "produce and market" since the former may sound threatening or impossible and the latter says it just as well.

When speaking at the professional gatherings, the recompense is usually the joy of speaking before colleagues. Sometimes concessions are made to allow book sales. So repeatedly pursuing this activity only makes sense, in an empire-building context, if there is some income-producing tie-in or follow-up.

If you are preparing the book *Computing and Electronics* (or whatever groups you name): *How To Sell Your Own Books, Texts, Tools, and Products*, that too would be an excellent seminar title for those directly involved or wanting to be. The seminar would have to be self-sponsored, or perhaps sponsored by organizations or associations from the field(s) covered. Since you know the mailing lists available in the field(s), fliers sent to those listed should attract eager participants.

How might these appear on your worksheet?

SEMINAR: TEACHERS/SELF-PUBLISHING, COLLEGE/UNI-VERSITY: based on full-day seminar to 20 participants at $65 (lunch excluded), 50% split with school: costs, negligible if distance near; profit, $650 plus back-of-the-room sales of $150-300.

PROGRAM ABOUT SELF-PUBLISHING AT CONFERENCE/CON-VENTION: cost, registration fee plus travel, room, and food (sometimes reimbursed); income, none or honorarium, plus back-of-room back sales if allowed ($50-200).

SEMINAR: COMPUTING AND ELECTRONICS FIELD, SELF-SPONSORED: based on full-day seminar being offered at four sites (New York, Chicago, L.A., and San Jose) to 20 particpants at $100 (lunch excluded): the costs, $4,350; projected income, $8,000; profit, from $3,000 loss to $3,650 gain, plus back-of-the-room sales of $1,000-2,200. Consulting spinoff.

"I in mine own house am an emperor
And will defend what is mine."

Massinger, *The Roman Actor* (1629)

"When a wallet grows, so do necessities."

Jewish folk saying

Thoughts and suggestions . . .

Professional Speaking

"It doesn't hurt to cite reputable sources. To mix in the company of Socrates, Lincoln, Twain, and Gandhi is good company indeed. It can't help but elevate an already solid speech."

"Never lie to an audience, straight out or by implication. That's a lesson that school teachers learn early in the game. The kids can tell. So can listeners, as much by the tone of your voice as the incredulity of your story."

Source: *Speaking For Money*

13

ACTION PLAN

Finally, a master plan for your empire!

You know the purpose of your empire and the expectations you have for it.

You have identified the basic needs to be met by that empire.

From the many goals you wish to achieve in your life you have selected one, restated it as an objective, and from it extracted a core subject that will provide the inspiration and fuel for the empire.

You know why you wish to pursue this objective, and, by extension, why it is worth all of the time and energy needed to create and establish your empire.

You have researched your core subject and developed a base of knowledge and a process by which you will keep that knowledge expanding and current.

You have identified those who want your information, the benefits that knowledge can bring them, and the means most appropriate for its transmission.

You have used various tools, like "gridding," "topic-spoking" and "topic-tiering," to expand the ways by which you can see and develop your core subject.

And you have taken all of this information and created various action paths by which you can most effectively realize your objective.

Yet action paths need specific markets to bring benefits to beneficiaries, so through that market identity you have been able to establish value and time priorities for the action paths.

Now you must convert the action paths, each with its many means and more markets, into a master action plan, with its own priorities. You must draw from the previous 12 steps to determine how you can both achieve your objective and satisfy your basic needs.

One way to do that is to determine the length of time by which your empire must fully meet your needs, then calculate the percentage of income it must provide, the costs it can incur, and the amount of available time you will have to put into the empire's development until that date.

Then you must select, from the many means of the action paths, those most likely to develop the best empire while still satisfying the variables mentioned. This may require more research to develop reliable data so you can make intelligent, and sometimes tough, choices.

The result is an action plan designed to carry you from the inception of the idea to its fullest fruition. From a thought and a perceived need to an empire that lets you share information about that idea and meet needs full time, and be well rewarded for having borne the yoke of development and identification so well for so long.

EXAMPLE

Choices, choices — and limits.

You have to remain in your present job for one year and squeeze in your empire-building activities around it.

You have enough money in reserve to work full-time on the empire for six months, but virtually no extra cash to pick up its costs.

You have a family and responsibilities so for those needs you require $42,000 the first year, $43,000 the next, and less than $50,000 the third.

You also want to build an empire that will show others how to self-publish, an empire known for excellence and honesty. It will have to earn your third year's needs plus pay its own expenses. So it will have to be fully functional in 24 months.

Those are the hoops and hurdles. What's new?

So what you must do is take a long, hard look at the action paths, the means, and the markets that you have identified in the last two steps, project them against your objective and your financial needs and resources, and create that no-nonsense, time-sequenced, prioritized action plan that will carry you from where you are to where you want to be by the time need requires you to be there.

For starters you set aside two means.

Video cassettes cost too much to create and market with scant or nonexistent resources. And consulting presumes knowledge about and experience with a topic, and at this stage that is what you are gathering and creating. So if consulting becomes a possibility, fine, but you won't actively seek it until stronger bases are established during the first two years.

You will focus your attention on articles, books, audio cassettes, seminars, a workshop, and a bit of mail order. Seminars and the book come first.

Seminars:

Since you are working an eight-hour day, you could offer seminars during the evening or on Saturdays or Sundays. And since you have no money to use, speculatively or at all, for the promotion required for self-sponsored seminars, you will turn to the colleges and universities to offer your programs under their extended education or community services sponsorship.

While the implementation steps will be described more fully in the next chapter, you must see what those schools need of what you know, design seminars to offer it, and sell them on booking you.

You study their catalogs and find three areas you think that others would pay to know more about. You limit the length of the programs to four hours and suggest that the school charge $45 per participant. The titles you pick are:

"How To Self-Publish Your Own Book"
"Mail Order: Part-Time Bonanza"
"Teachers: Why Aren't You Selling What You Know?"

Your goal is to offer each of the three at five different schools (of the 12 within 80 miles driving distance), or 15 seminars during the second half of the year. Estimating 20 participants at each and a 50% split of the gross with the schools, that would bring $6,750 income.

If you select three or four top books about the subjects to sell after the program, and calculate a gross of $10 a person, your profit (about 1/3 of the book's list price) would be an additional $990. Add the $990 to the $6,750 from the seminars and your gross would be $7,740. Subtract the $740 for costs (workbooks, travel, food, book shipping, etc.) and you have some $7,000 for the living kitty.

You'll plan to reschedule those seminars, or others similar, during the second year as well, and continue doing so until other means become more important to your evolving empire.

Book:

Your major activity that first year is the planning, designing, and writing of a book.

Good books about self-publishing exist — those by Poynter and the Rosses are excellent — but you see where an even better book is needed. You propose a guidebook that explains what the reader does by taking him or her through each step, with forms and models at hand. Moreover, your book will begin with the marketing: the identification of the buyer or user, an analysis of their needs, a study of the other books available to see how they meet those needs, your determination of the book's unique feature(s), and a projection of how the book will be part of the reader's empire.

Then your book will show how the reader designs the book to fully meet the buyer's and their own needs. From the content and cover design, it will discuss content preparation, early promotion, book production, full promotion, distribution, spinoffs, revision plan, and much more. Your book will feature one example throughout: itself as it was put together, as an example in hand of what it preaches! Thus you have a blueprint for the preparation of your book: the same you will be selling to others!

At this stage you use the calculations gathered in Step 12 (in a means analysis not reported in this text). You project publishing 3,500 copies, paperback, of a 304-page book that will sell for $14.95 each, for $52,325 gross income. Estimated costs of preparation, printing, and shipping are $11,575; $6,500 for promotion, and $11,456 from a discount of 50% for half of the books, leaving a maximum net income of $34,369.

By the end of the first year you plan to have the book at the printer's. You pay the typesetting and cover from your seminar earnings. For the printing, you pay half in advance, from the seminar income, and the rest 30 days later from seminars, article earnings, and from your savings.

Since you are writing about book preparation and promotion, the steps you follow are in front of you. By using the same clever techniques you are sharing with the book's readers, you expect to replace the savings used as well as to earn most of the funds needed for the second year from the book's income.

The hardest thing will be sticking to a firm book preparation schedule. So you plan to work 90 minutes a day, uninterrupted, and adhere strictly to a production timetable you will devise. In fact, you plan to rise 90 minutes earlier each morning, before the distractions appear. The rest of the free time is for seminars, articles, tapes, and family, by the most pressing order!

Articles:

While you are gathering information for the book, you plan to follow up on some of the better magazine markets selected in Step 12, figure out appropriate slants to the readers of those magazines, and query the editor. Your goal is to sell six articles at $350 average income, then earn an additional $600 from reprints of those sales, for a total of $2,700. Your article-writing will be saved until the second half of the first year, after your book's basic research is completed. A time-filler when you're not offering seminars.

Audio Cassettes:

The final activity of the first year will be the taping of each seminar to offer for sale as series, three 60-minutes tapes each of the respective programs, labelled and packaged in vinyl albums, with a copy of the same workbook distributed at the seminars. These will cost what the seminars cost, minus a nickel. If the seminars cost $45, the series, $44.95. And they will be offered for two reasons: (1) for those unfortunate souls unable to see and hear you in person but nonetheless desperately in need of your message, and (2) those who did hear you but want to inflict like harm on their friends by tape -- or themselves again! (Your promotion will describe the benefits somewhat differently.)

Rather than pay outsiders to tape you live, for which you have too little money, or fumble through it yourself, these will be taped on a borrowed, rented, or bought tape deck, with a microphone, at your home studio — the garage, attic, or padded room. More details in Step 14.

So much for the first year. You are working and eating on those earnings, plus saving $6,000 for the second-year kitty. Your days and nights are packed solid with empire-building activity. The next year is when it really gets chaotic!

THE SECOND YEAR

You have enough money to survive at least half a year, between savings and other resources. So you decide to work three more months — until April 1. You also have a sizable accumulation of sick and vacation time. If your employer will convert that to cash, you will work until April 1; if not, you will deduct the due days from April 1 and begin empire-building full-time the moment you can.

Your **book** arrives as the second year begins! You have boxes delivered to your distributors and comp copies sent to the reviewers, and you do all of the things you explained to the book's readers to get the public to buy this exciting new release. You also sell it back-of-the-room at your seminars, replacing other books it resembles. That will triple the take home income from each item sold.

You continue offering **seminars**, expecting another $6,750 during the second year, plus some $2,000 from book sales, with your book and audio cassettes now available. As material for new **articles** appears, you continue to query and produce salable pieces, though at this point you cite your book in the text, if appropriate, or at least mention it (with cost and ordering address) in the author's biographical insert.

Mail Order:

Now that you have products that others want, you set up a means for mail order fulfillment. At the seminars you include a flyer with the workbook offering to provide, by mail, your book(s), tape albums, and others books about related subjects. In each copy of your book, in the back, is a similar order form for your products. And every time you correspond with an interested person, speak to a group, or somehow acquire addresses of those who would benefit, you give them a flyer or mail one to them.

Profitable? You bet. You figure on selling at least $2,000 net without any directed mailings, and much more with them. Alas, you hold off on the mailings until the next items in your selling arsenal become available: the case study books.

Case Study Books:

Your first book, about self-publishing, is a basic how-to text applicable for virtually all forms of books, booklets, manuals, whatever.

To supplement that you produce six more books during your second year, two every three months beginning in June. At 160 pages each and costing $9.95, each book will feature three fact-filled, step-by-step case studies based on true examples.

The first two books would be for teachers (with an example of a worksheet throwaway book, a personal journal workbook, and a textbook) and poets (three kinds of poetry books: children's illustrated, adult with line drawings, and long adult without illustrations).

The second two would be for speakers (detailed workbook, key theme book, resources book) and about business (desk organizer/journal, process book, textbook). And the third set, for family historians (biography, collected memoirs, family tree and roots) and for communications teachers (designed to be used in class, with facts needed from which students could draw to create their own model book; exercises throughout).

You publish 2,000 copies of each, in paper, costing you $4,400 per book, plus $1,500 for promotion and $4,975 for 50% discounting of 25% of the total, and you have a maximum potential profit of $13,425 each. That means $54,150 for six. Which is the source of your survival during the third year!

The value of the case study books? To fully understand them the basic text, with its unique structure, is necessary. So they help sell the basic text. And anybody eager to self-publish who has the basic text will want to see at least one case study, and probably more. They add additional back-of-the-room sales items to your seminar table, more to hawk by mail order, more article material to rework for print — and they help people, which is what it's all about anyway!

You needn't stop at six. Nor must the format be solely of case studies, as the volume for communications instructors shows.

Workshop:

One more activity begins in the second year: the creation of a workshop to be offered in-house at businesses and corporations. The thrust is three-fold, with the most appropriate of the three designed and presented to the booker. One topic is in-house publishing, another, manual preparation, and the third, newsletter preparation.

Estimated income from the workshop is $1,000, with costs absorbed in the contract. Three workshops are the goal for the latter half of the second year, with some of the leads for the companies picked up from participants at the seminars or those seeking consulting advice stemming from the book or case studies.

Mailing List:

Finally, you are compiling a mailing list from seminar participants, book buyers (from the order flyer on the last page), and anybody directly in contact with you in some self-publishing context. This you code by year and kind of activity or contact. You use the list for your own mail order needs and to rent to others. Alas, the list is still so small it doesn't yet figure in your income tally.

THE THIRD YEAR

The idea was to define your core subject, develop outward from it, help others, establish your expertise, and create a permanent income base. You're right on target with your objective clearly in view!

You have already put in motion most of the means of information dissemination — articles, books, tapes, seminars, and workshops — and will be consulting much more in your third year. And when or if video cassettes enhance your sharing, they too will come on line.

In your third and fourth year you see five directions for growth.

The first: consolidate and evaluate what you are already doing. Expand and contract according to the perceived need.

The second: more case studies.

The third: case study books with a different purpose. These focus in detail on specific elements of self-publishing: research, cover design, financing, promotion, co-authoring, book selling, the business of self-publishing, indexing and proofing, desktop tools, book clubs, and so on.

The fourth: services. Beyond consulting, many self-publishers want or need the direct involvement of others at the professional level. This includes editing, proofing, rewriting, design, marketing plan preparation, teletypesetting, layout, pasteup, board preparation, printing, fulfillment, and more.

The fifth: publishing others' books.

Your empire is up and earning — on paper! The action plan looks exciting, exhausting, invigorating, demanding, extremely beneficial to others, extremely demanding of you. What's new?

Now you must take the first steps to actually put the plan in motion.

"Knowledge is of two kinds. We know a subject ourselves, or we know where we can find information upon it."

Samuel Johnson, 1775

"Sad is the man who has nothing but money."

Jewish folk saying

14

IMPLEMENTATION

To implement is to fulfill or accomplish. It is to take the plan and turn it into reality, to put action in motion.

Yet marathons aren't run in one fast step, nor are empires built in a single swoop. Implementation in this context means first breaking the plan into achievable portions, then moving forward to realize the greater whole.

So you must now isolate those acts to be accomplished first, determine precisely how they are performed, and methodically do them, and then do the same to each act that follows.

Fortunately, in idea dissemination the means are neither mysterious nor unknown. People successfully and regularly write articles and books, they repeatedly offer enlightening seminars and audience-lifting speeches. The techniques for success in each field are known and shared in print.

This book's bibliography recommends many books and tapes that are practical and applied in nature. Most are straightforward, virtually step-by-step guides. The empire-builder has only to muster up the courage, read, listen, study others, ask about, then develop or tune up skills, and do. Success is copiable and contagious. But not instant.

One purpose of this book is to explain how you reach the stage of implementation, then, briefly, what you do, in a process sense, at and after it. Yet implementation is far from being as predictable and instructable as that sounds.

In the world of information dissemination, nothing — action plans included — goes entirely as planned. Your plan suggests an ideal course of action, at least at the time of its preparation. It doesn't call for flexibility: why would you consider changing the best plan you could create?

But flexibility is very much called for. If your action plan proves impractical, or even impossible, to implement, the same wisdom that helped you design that plan must be called upon to find the next best mode of operation.

If, in the process of implementation, you see an even better way to realize your objective, weigh it seriously and change if wisdom so rules.

There are also times when, in completing one step of the plan, an ounce more of activity will produce a pound more of results. For example, in writing an article the same basic material can be often be rewritten into how-to fillers; that extra hour could result in positive exposure before thousands more eyes.

All of which means that a plan is a plan, to be held to unless its carrying through can be done even better, or with more positive results. Adhere to the spirit and the purpose of the plan but improve it if you can.

Implementation is mainly taking the first, then the second, and finally the last step of making the intent of the plan come true. The first thirteen steps provide the depth of knowledge and process to allow you to act, or improvise, intelligently at this crucial phase.

EXAMPLE:

Implementation means laying out the first steps for the next few months while keeping the plan's direction and intent for the next year or two in view.

For your self-publishing empire the first means in question are seminars, a book, then audio cassettes and magazines. So you review the books or tapes that explain the organizational process for each, adapt the information to your subject and situation, and list the things you must do now or soon.

Your lists are as follows:

Seminars:

1. Contact all of the colleges and universities within 80 miles and request a catalog of their coming extended education or community service seminars or workshops.
2. Study the section(s) where your seminars would be listed. Focus on the seminar closest to your offerings. Determine which schools aren't offering similar programs as well as those where your seminar could be modified in title and form to complement another that is related.
3. Note the name, title, address of each school's director.
4. For each seminar that you want to offer prepare a description that is 3-5 short paragraphs long, with a "bulletin" insert explaining the benefits or points covered. It should also include the length of the seminar, suggested cost to the participant, and your address and Social Security number.
5. Prepare a resume or biographical excerpt for use with the description.
6. Prepare a seminar outline.
7. Make clean copies of the items prepared and send them to each program director with a letter of introduction that explains that you would like to offer the seminars described through the college or university, why people would register to hear the seminar, what qualifications you have, and a suggested date or two. Send this at least four, preferably six, months prior to the first date.
8. When booked, prepare the script for that seminar.
9. After the script is finished, prepare a workbook that will help the participant better understand the presentation and expand their information base, to keep for later reference.
10. Prepare a sufficient number of copies of the workbook.

Book:

1. Keep detailed notes about the exact process followed plus copies of all forms used in the preparation of your book since it uses its own preparation as the text's example!
2. Identify who would buy or use a book about self-publishing.
3. List the buyer or user's needs. What benefits would they receive from this book?
4. What needs must you meet by preparing the book?
5. How can the buyer/user's needs and yours be better met through the design of this book? The cover? The layout? Type? Leading?
6. How can the contents be organized to best meet the buyer's and your needs?
7. Design the cover or have that begun by a qualified specialist.
8. Begin the research and copy gathering for the book's contents.

Articles:

1. List all of the article markets from Step 12; note the topic or angle that provoked each listing.
2. List additional magazines and newsletters as they come to mind or you find information about or reference to them. Write the topic or angle best matched to the market. Combine and prioritize the lists from (1.) and (2.).
3. In gathering information for your book, if it matches your topic or angles for the top markets on your combined list, query the editor about an article.
4. If the editor is interested, study the publication closely, find more material, and write the article.

Audio Cassettes:

1. Offer each seminar several times, modifying and improving the script.
2. Borrow, rent, or buy a tape deck that produces clear tapes.
3. List all of the tape duplicators in your area, plus others recommended from other areas. Check rates, delivery times, other services offered, studio availability, recommendations.

4. Locate label printers. Get price list, delivery time. Have labels printed.
5. List all audio tape album and single-box suppliers. Check prices, delivery schedules, other services offered, recommendations. Buy albums.
6. Design album cover insert or screen artwork. Bid with local printers or graphic artists. Have artwork done. Insert in album.
7. Tape each seminar presentation live. Study sound and content. Modify script for preparing your master tape.
8. Tape entire seminar with tape deck at home.
9. If you wish, have studio edit introduction or other sounds into masters.
10. Listen to masters. Make final changes. Have duplications of masters made.
11. Label the cassettes and insert in albums, for sale.

Back-of-the-Room Products:

1. Select the best books in the fields about which you are seminaring. Which of these will be particularly helpful to the participants?
2. Contact the publishers of the most helpful: request a commercial discount sheet and credit reference forms.
3. Can the participants afford the books at retail rate?
4. If so, select three or four of the best and order enough to sell back of the room at your seminars. Check return policy.
5. Prepare an order form for use at the seminars.
6. Check your bank to arrange VISA/Master Charge. If you decide to offer the service, put appropriate fill-in material on the order forms.
7. Prepare an order form that describes the books more fully that the seminar participant can take home for ordering later.
8. Get a state resale number before selling books or products.

Get the idea? Checklists to get going, to implement the action plan. When one checklist is finished, another is begun. And so it goes, until the empire is up, operating, and the implementation is complete!

Thoughts and suggestions . . .

Choosing a Seminar Subject

While there are thousands of kinds of seminars, to succeed they must all do the same thing: meet a need and satisfy it.

People will pay, in money and time, to receive benefits. A need met and satisfied is a benefit received. Investing wisely, confronting shyness, learning to love, properly pruning pear trees, writing sonnets, taming your IBM — all are flowers, each a slightly different shade of green.

Source: *How To Set Up and Market Your Own Seminar*

15.

REVIEW

E mpires are like beauty, defined by the beholder. There are no absolutes. They can always be bigger, stronger, more widely spread; they can always do better what they are supposed to do, or make more money, or help more people.

And emperors change. Between the dream and reality comes learning, maturity, tolerance, new tools, better skills. So what was right and seemingly the only way at one point becomes quaint and ill-advised later. The need for review and change is constant, from the day the empire begins until the day it ends.

That's what makes life hard in this era of relativity. Your ancestors knew how to hunt because that's how their ancestors hunted. But civilization intervened, and with it the widespread acceptance of choices, and you are caught with the confusing consequences when you attempt to apply choices to your own life.

It is impossible to write a book of 15, or 115, steps that require no interpretation and that will always result in a perfect empire, as impossible as giving you a 15-step recipe that would always result in a perfect pie. Instead, the 15 steps in this book are full of variables that can be interpreted 1,115 ways and that could result in a million different pies, ranging from delicious to poisonous.

The value, on the other hand, of such choices is the difference between the life of the primitives and what you see about you today. And the possibility that you, innately bestowed with the same tools as your friends, can create an empire, your own, designed to fill your dreams as fully and in the way you want them filled, while your friends can do the same. And no two empires will be alike!

The second value is that once you begin the empire's quest you can change directions, means, resources, tools — any element is open to change — as long as that change results in better achieving your goal. You can even change that goal, but at greater peril, for a goal change requires a re-evaluation of all that has been done up to that point and projected into the future, to bring the old goal and the new into attainable harmony.

How do you stay on course and correct the sails? Write your objective, your goal, on a sheet of paper, enlarge it, make a dozen copies, and post them within sight in every room, at every desk, near every computer — so you are constantly sailing in your chosen direction.

Then make a date with yourself every three months — put it on your calendar — to take a day off (or, in the beginning, when you may still be working for somebody else, an evening off) and isolate yourself, to review, step-by-step, where you are headed, how you are getting there, where improvements are required or desirable, how you can do better what you are doing now. Use that day to review the steps in this book, to update your "topic-spoking," to research, to talk with others. One day (or evening) in 90 to check the maps and adjust your course.

You're not a sailor afloat in an indifferent sea. You're the admiral, the emperor of the seas. It's your ship, you set the goal and keep your own schedule. You're in charge. Check your ship daily. Make repairs regularly. Plot voyages annually. But when the seas roll or the doldrums attack, review and act. It's your ship.

It's your empire. From one idea, through writing and speaking, you can build the kind of life you desire. Nobody else will build it for you.

It takes clarity of vision, hard work, planning, creativity, and perseverance — all traits you already possess. Now you must apply them.

This book suggests 15 steps by which you can build that empire. A plan from which you can draw a blueprint and lay the bricks. So get going — empires aren't instant and you're only alive once. Get out a sheet of paper and start at Step 1: what **do** you want to do with your life?

"The day of small nations has long passed away. The day of Empires has come."

Joseph Chamberlain, 1904

PART
FIVE

Assorted Guides

Assorted Guidelines

T o fully understand how to use each of the means of information dissemination would take many books, extensive study, and diligent application. The inclusion here of selected guidelines for some of the key means, therefore, is offered only as an aid, and the reader is directed to the bibliography for further assistance.

Articles

Often the most penetrating means of dissemination is an article in a magazine or newspaper, particularly one specifically directed to a publication read by the prime beneficiaries.

Writing such an article can be a major task, but for the literate who are knowledgeable about the subject and who closely study other articles in print, it is doable. Persuading an editor to put the words in print can be even more difficult.

So four article-related items are included in Part Five, as guides to action. Each is somewhat self-explanatory, with the source also indicated should the reader desire further explanation.

The first is a "formula" for increasing the chances of having an article accepted while decreasing the time spent on its preparation and placement, followed by a flow chart called "The Mechanics of Getting Into Print." Next, "How To Prepare and Market Articles That Sell." The fourth, "How To Study a Printed Magazine Article," shows how one uses items in print as teaching tools for preparing their own articles for the same or similar publications.

THE MECHANICS OF GETTING INTO PRINT

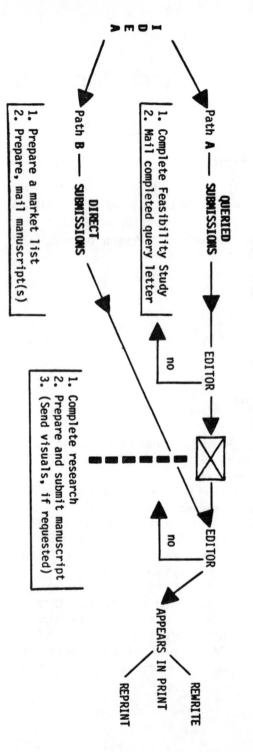

IDEA

Path A — QUERIED SUBMISSIONS

1. Complete Feasibility Study
2. Mail completed query letter

EDITOR → (no)

Path B — DIRECT SUBMISSIONS

1. Prepare a market list
2. Prepare, mail manuscript(s)

EDITOR → (no)

1. Complete research
2. Prepare and submit manuscript
3. (Send visuals, if requested)

APPEARS IN PRINT

REWRITE

REPRINT

Path **A** is for most nonfiction articles and books; includes humorous (where humor is the style rather than purpose).

Path **B** is for simultaneous submissions as well as fiction, fillers, and humor (where humor is the purpose).

Source: *Query Letters/Cover Letters: How They Sell Your Writing.*

How To Prepare and Market Articles That Sell

(1.) In one sentence, what is the subject of the article you want to write and sell?

(2.) Who would benefit from reading your article? Who would be most interested? What kinds of readers would select your specific subject from a variety of choices? Rank all of those potential readers in order with those who would derive the most benefits first.

(3.) Which publications do these readers buy and read? Prepare a market list of those publications that are the most likely to buy your manuscript.

(4.) In addition to the publications checked in (3.), it is necessary to review the broader publishing field for articles similar or identical to yours. Therefore, you must check both the *Reader's Guide to Periodical Literature* and the specific subject indexes for at least three previous years, then

---

"If a query does its job, I have a good idea what the article will be like and the chances of its being rejected are almost nil. But a query to do its job must give me a good idea of how the subject will be covered, how well the writer uses the language, and how much editing I will have to do on the manuscript."

Bill Sonneborn, Editor, *Michiana* Magazine, of *The South Bend Tribune*

    (a) list the articles that are closest to your subject, in order with the most similar first: subject, author, title, publication, page reference, length, and when they appeared. Where the subjects appear to be very similar, how does yours differ?

    (b) cross-check newspaper indexes for the past three years and provide the same information.

(5.) Have the publications listed in (3. and 4.) printed articles within the past three years that are similar to the one you propose?

(6.) After each publication note the name of the person you should contact (editor, managing editor, etc.), with title and address. Then provide the following information about each publication:

    (a) does it pay on acceptance or publication?

    (b) how much does it pay for articles as long as yours?

    (c) does it prefer a query or a direct submission?

    (d) how often is it published?

    (e) what percentage of it is written by freelancers?

    (f) what is its preferred manuscript length?

    (g) is any other information provided that will affect its placement on your list?

(7.) Now rank your market list in priority order, based on when the buyers pay (acceptance/publication), how much, the frequency of publication, and the percentage of freelance material used per issue.

(8.) Read the latest issues of your target publication, front to back. Select the articles that are the most similar, in form if not topic, to the piece you will prepare. Outline each article. Write out the lead and conclusion of each, by hand. Attempt to identify the publication's readers by age, sex, occupation, income range, education, residence, and other pertinent factors.

(9.) To verify the availability of resource information

    (a) read as many of the articles in (5.) as necessary or possible, then list the sources of information found in each,

    (b) go to the library and consult the card catalog and list books to which you will refer for factual information: title, author, call number, date of publication, and

    (c) list the human resources you should consult for additional information and quotes, working with the reference librarian for information that you do not already have: their names, positions and current affiliations (if related to the topic), academic titles and degrees (if relevant), and reasons for their being consulted.

(10.) From the researched and specific target publication information gathered, select the material needed to write a professional query letter. Verify its accuracy.

(11.) Write a selling query letter to an editor of your target publication. If you do not receive a positive reply, write a query letter to the editor of the next publication on your list, and so on, one editor at a time, until an editor does respond positively. Repeat as much of (9.) as necessary for each new publication queried.

(12.) When you receive that positive response to your query, plan your article to determine what is still needed for its completion.

(13.) Complete the needed research.

(14.) Write the manuscript in final draft form. Include, on separate paper, at least five additional, different leads.

(15.) Select the best lead, edit the draft, type a final manuscript (keeping a copy), and mail it, with illustrations (if available and needed), to the editor of your target publication.

Ten of the fifteen steps *precede* the query letter. You must first find something to write about, decide whether it's feasible to complete an article about that topic, and whether there are markets with readers eager for your information.

Then you query. You send a letter to the editor of the most likely publication. If you get a negative reply, you try the second editor, and down the list, one at a time, until a publishing genius recognizes your talents and a gripping topic and says "yes, I'll look at it!" Only then do you fully research, interview, photo, and write.

Source: *Query Letters/Cover Letters: How They Sell Your Writing."*

The "Formula"

"Write only when you have better than a 50% chance of a sale and, once sold, sell reprints and rewrites of the same material."

"You have better than a 50% chance of a sale by querying, and writing once you have a positive response to your query, or by writing to markets where you can simultaneously submit the same material."

Source: *How To Sell 75% of Your Freelance Writing."*

How To Study a Printed Magazine Article

(1.) Read the article closely, then ask yourself what basic or working question it answers. Write the question out. It may also answer secondary questions, so write those out too.

(2.) Now read the write-up for that publication in the *Writer's Market* for the year of (or preceding) the article's appearance. Given the working question in (1) and the indications in the *Writer's Market* of what that magazine was seeking, try to put yourself in the writer's shoes. How did the writer slant the subject to appeal to the magazine's readers? Why did the editor buy it? Study its length, illustrations, position in the magazine.

(3.) To see how the writer carries the main theme through the article, underline each word that relates directly to that theme, then outline the entire piece. Study the writer's use of facts, quotes, and anecdotes. What is the ratio between them? How is humor used? Is it spread and balanced to the same degree throughout? Do other articles in this issue use facts, quotes, anecdotes, and humor in roughly the same way and in the same proportion?

(4.) List every source used, including direct references and quotations. Where would the writer find the facts, opinions, and quotes that are not clearly identified by source in the article? If you are uncertain, indicate where you might find the material — or where you would go to find out.

(5.) Focus on the quotations. Why is each used? How does it carry the theme forward? Note how the source of the quotation is introduced, and how much the reader must know about the source to place the person and what is said into perspective.

(6.) Is the article written in first person (I), second (you), or third (he, she, or it)? How does that strengthen the article? Does the person change? Why or why not? Are most other articles in the same issue written in the same person?

(7.) Set the title aside and concentrate on the lead. How long is it, in words or sentences? How does it grab your interest? Does it make you want to read more? Why? How does it compare with other leads in that issue?

(8.) Most articles begin with a short lead followed by a longer second or third paragraph that ties the lead to the body of the article. Called the transitional paragraph, it tells where you are going and how you will get there. It bridges the attention-grabbing elements of the lead to the expository elements of the body by setting direction, tone, and pace. Find the transitional paragraph and study it. Organizationally, after the lead it is the most important item in the article.

(9.)   Now underline the first sentence in each paragraph. They should provide a rough chain that will pull you through the piece. Note how the writer draws the paragraphs together with transitional words and phrases. Circle the words that perform this linking function. Often the same words or ideas will be repeated in the last sentence of one paragraph and the first sentence of the next.

(10.)   Earlier you outlined the article. Now look at the transitional words and the underlined first sentences and see how the structure ties the theme together. Is the article structured chronologically, developmentally, by alternating examples, point-by-point? Or if the article was written to answer the working question you isolated in (1), did the answers to the secondary questions stemming from that working question provide the article's organizational structure?

(11.)   How does the article end? Does it tie back to the lead? Does it repeat an opening phrase or idea? The conclusion should reinforce and strengthen the direction the article has taken. Does it? How?

(12.)   Finally, look at the title. It may have been changed or rewritten by the editor. Nonetheless, does it correctly describe the article that follows? Does it tease, quote, pique one's curiosity, state facts? What technique does it use to make the reader want to read the article?

Source: *How To Sell 75% of Your Freelance Writing."*

Books

Books represent a much greater investment of time and energy than articles, though they are, paradoxically, easier to put in print.

Empire-building books are far more likely to be nonfiction than fiction, at least by intent. And publishers are far more receptive to publishing that form of issue. An alternative, by choice or default, is the very topic of our example: self-publishing. So putting a book on paper and in a buyer's hand isn't difficult. Writing it is.

This text talks at length about self-publishing, and the best books describing the process, so there is no purpose to repeating those words again.

As for selecting and convincing an established publisher to publish and properly promote your book, the process is quite similar to that just described for articles. You study the field to see what else is in print, research your topic, see which publishers specialize in that subject, select the best for your needs, write a full (two-page) query letter that sells your idea and you as the person to write about it, append other necessary information to that letter (annotated table of contents or outline, one-page synopsis, reference/resource sheet, etc.), and (usually) write several chapters after receiving a positive response from the editor.

The bibliography indicates several tools that will help you through this process. The greatest value of book writing for empire-building? Probably the validation of expertise that good ideas well organized and written to book length can bring.

Seminars

Two means are the best engines for an empire-building train: seminars and books. That is, from them many other means can be developed or dispensed. From books come articles, the core for tapes, the research for seminars, and so on . . .

From seminars come a physical and mental display of information dissemination: speaking skill and organization displayed, products sold back of the room, consulting arranged, and much more.

The main problem with seminars is getting people to attend — and pay for the honor! So the first item is called a "Five-Step Guide for Seminar Success." The second, a "Seminar Organizational Schedule."

Five-Step Guide for Seminar Success

The following guide will serve as a checklist for those organizing seminars as well as a review for those already practicing the trade. They are specifically applicable to public seminars, since most seminar-givers begin in the public realm. With slight modification, however, they can apply to all seminars, however organized or financed.

(1.) *The subject must be appealing and clearly stated in the title and description, plus it must meet a need sufficiently strong that one will pay to attend.*

That is, the person must be attracted to the subject by the title, which is reinforced and expanded in the description. He must see the seminar as a way to meet a need. It must be clear why he should attend. The benefits must be stated or obvious: by attending the seminar he will solve personal problems, get rich, learn a skill that will ultimately result in a raise or a more responsible position, find security, overcome frustrations, improve his sex life, . . .

This is the single most important guideline of the five. The best promotion, finest location, and most attractive fee imaginable will not sell a senseless title or a garbled, pointless description any more than you would believe a man dressed in tatters, with manure on his shoes and food in his hair, who told you that, for a fee and a few hours of your time, he would show you how to become rich and successful.

(2.) *The seminar must be scheduled when and where the public will attend.*

Naturally, you say. That's obvious. But how many have tried to offer seminars about personal safety at nighttime — the very hours when those most worried about their safety won't leave their homes? Or seminars that teach how to make your boss richer, by improving your skills or efficiency, during your nonworking hours?

If you are offering a seminar that shows how to instantly turn marbles into rubies, you can charge a bundle, give it atop a mountain at 3 a.m., and throw in a whip-toothed rainstorm to test the participants' mettle. The throngs would joyously haul their glass spheroids to wherever you are whenever you speak!

But most of us offer programs markedly less glittering. To us the time and place are proportionately more important to our seminar's success.

(3.) *The cost must be in line with perceived benefits and other ways of realizing those benefits.*

"Perceived" is the key word. The benefits can be there but if one doesn't perceive them — why they are worth having or that they can be gained from your seminar — any cost will be too high.

Assuming that the benefits are not only perceived, they are desired, then your seminar must be affordable and in line with other means of getting those benefits. For example, if your seminar costs $100 and one virtually identical costs $35, where do you think the participants will go? On the other hand, if you are explaining a crucial "how-to" link absolutely necessary to securing $10,000 contracts and yours is the only program fully sharing that information, isn't a fee of $500 or more worth the investment?

Your main competition is other seminars, and sometimes wildcat consultants. Rarely will taped programs have more appeal than a live presentation, and books, though they may cost only a fraction as much, will be a factor only when your seminar is considered marginal by the participants, when your audience is already book-oriented, or when it is highly price-conscious. Very few will opt to attend a class lasting from several to many weeks when they feel that a seminar can cover the core material adequately.

(4.) *The participant must know of the seminar's existence and be attracted to it.*

If one has an idea that is salable as a seminar, promotion is usually the difference between success or failure. For though it may be the best idea imaginable, a foolproof way to solve the most pressing need, if nobody knows about it who will attend? Without promotion, who will read the title and description and hurry to register before the hall fills?

Yet promotion is also the greatest financial risk. Self-promoted seminars often take as much as two-thirds of their anticipated income to attract registrants before a penny is made. Promotion properly done can draw crowds to seminars that are promotable. But if the topic, title, description, timing, location, and all the rest aren't right, that is, if the seminar isn't promotable, all of the costs spent making your seminar known may be useless — or at least ultimately profitless.

So here's where the dice are thrown and the gamble is made: promotional means content, cost, and repetition. All seminars must be promotable. All must be promoted. The rest is risk.

(5.) *The seminar's content and your presentation are crucial for long-term success.*

If you are going to offer the seminar time and again — and why would you go to so much trouble if you weren't? — what you say and how you say it will be its own best long-term promotion.

Neither the actual content nor your presentation will attract participants to your first seminar. They will register by what you tell them you will say: by the title, description, and the promotional promises. Like a book, first-timers buy seminars by the cover. They don't know if you're a bumbler or have a tongue of honey. They buy on faith.

But if you don't come through, your future is tainted, for nothing is more forceful or harder to erase than negative word-of-mouth.

Therefore, the first time out you must provide not only solid content and professional presentation, particular attention must be paid to the first four steps of this guide so that the number of bearers of positive word-of-mouth is large. Over time the content and presentation, if good, will reduce the risk of promotion and will provide the desired cushion of profit, as long as the first three steps in this guide are properly tended to.

In the business realm, content and presentation are particularly critical from the outset. The first question a potential programmer will ask is "Where did you give this seminar before?" Those references will then be asked, "Is he any good?" And you will be booked primarily from the responses of those who heard you perform. Businesses don't take the risks that the public must. Thus the first business booking is extremely hard to get. Later bookings are far easier when that reply is, "He's super. The best money you'll ever spend." That's why content and presentation, properly done, are money in the bank.

Source: *Speaking For Money."*

Seminar Organizational Schedule

The following list, of the keys steps of organizing and programming a seminar, is in rough chronological order.

(1.) Write a one-sentence topic for a seminar.

(2.) Concerning that topic, answer the following questions: Who cares? What problems will your seminar solve? How else can the same information be found? How much time or money would the participant save by attending your seminar? Why else would people attend it? Do other seminars about your topic exist? How much do they cost? How do they approach the topic? How long do they last? How often are they given? Where/how are they booked? Are they subsidized?

(3.) Write a seminar description that includes objectives, benefits, who should attend, and why.

(4.) Write a dozen titles. Select the best.

(5.) Evaluate the resources for your seminar preparation. While checking those resources, compile a bibliography for your workbook. Later, in using the resources, select the best and annotate them.

(6.) Prepare your budget: itemize expected costs and estimate when the money will be needed; list the possible unexpected costs by source and date; list anticipated income and when expected; plot your income and costs on a calendar;evaluate your need for a reserve fund, the amount and when needed; list your financial reserves: amount and when available; list the ways to increase income and reduce costs; determine the method(s) of participant payment: pre-registration only, discount for preregistration, higher fee at the door, cash or credit cards, etc.

(7.) Determine the minimum payment that you will accept for offering the seminar, factor in the cost of its presentation, then establish its cost to the participant.

(8.) Plan your speaking schedule: dates, hours, cities, sites; check feasibility of travel as scheduled; contact sites, book facilities, make hotel/motel reservations.

(9.) Plan your promotional campaign: list target audience, from the most to least likely to attend; list ways to make the seminar known, how to best appeal to each potential audience; establish an operational budget for the most effective promotional approaches; prepare the time/method list for promotional activities; implement your campaign.

(10.) Determine who will be your local contact at sites; establish responsibilities, method of reporting results; devise a method for recording, posting names of registrants to your mailing list; provide all needed promotional materials to your contact; determine who will handle and help with door registration, product sale, etc.

(11.) Determine the kind/amount of non-promotional printed material needed: workbooks, evaluation sheets, door registration forms, receipts, product sales forms; set up a production schedule: writing, typing or typesetting, pasteup, printing.

(12.) Prepare your seminar; plan, integrate audio-visual aids into the presentation; arrange for and schedule any outside speakers; evaluate your need for your own microphone, amplification, projectors, etc.; practice your presentation, opening and closing remarks; break the seminar into segments, schedule breaks.

(13.) Plan and purchase speaking attire that visually reinforces the seminar's objective.

(14.) As the day approaches for final cancellation of facility fee for full/partial refund, decide if the seminar will be given.

(15.) Review all promotional activities as the presentation day approaches.

(16.) If scheduled, give radio/TV and newspaper interviews.

(17.) Check the presentation site, the day before if possible; review the activities and provisions needed for the site personnel.

(18.) Arrive at least an hour before the seminar, set up equipment, review the activities/responsibilities of the helpers, dress.

(19.) Smile, take a deep breath, and give a super seminar!

(20.) Read the evaluation sheets to see how the next seminar can be even better!

Some Business Considerations

(a) Select a business name.

(b) Complete the fictitious business statement process.

(c) Get necessary city/state licenses; if selling a product, get resale number from state taxing board.

(d) Open business bank account.

(e) Check into credit card use at bank for registration/sale of products.

(f) Stock business stationery and needed supplies.

(g) Investigate joining business or professional associations.

(h) Familiarize yourself with single proprietorship and receipting responsibilities.

(i) Keep records and receipts for all income and expenses.

When Scheduling Through Academic Extension

(a)   Contact colleges/universities at least four months prior to the start of the quarter/semester to present your seminar(s) and yourself for possible inclusion in the next program, sending the title and description plus an outline of each seminar, a list of likely participants (by kind, vocation, description), and a resume — with a cover letter.

(b)   Offer to assist with promotion: news release preparation, radio/TV spots, etc.

(c)   Coordinate your workbook preparation with the extension office.

(d)   Prepare the necessary paperwork for later payment.

(e)   Maintain contact with each school prior to travelling there to offer seminars.

(f)   Familiarize yourself with door registration procedures and evaluation forms.

(g)   Return all funds and forms to the sponsoring school promptly after offering seminars.

Source: *"How To Set Up and Market Your Own Seminar."*

NOTES

NOTES

NOTES

NOTES

Bibliography

Since my publishing firm has focussed exclusively on empire-building and the related means for the past decade, it is not surprising that many of the items listed below are our books and tape series. Alas, we don't have the market cornered nor is there a shortage of other good books about the various means of dissemination, as you will see, though there is no other book, until this, that specifically talks about empire-building by writing and speaking.

To be listed a book must meet a second, and somewhat subjective criterion: it must be a no-nonsense, applied, how-to book that shows how to put theory into action.

Our products most directly related to empire-building will be listed first, with ordering information on the last page; those of our esteemed and valued colleagues in this exciting world, next, in greater detail.

Books:

Query Letters/Cover Letters: How They Sell Your Writing, 1986.
Speaking For Money, 1985.
How To Sell 75% of Your Freelance Writing, 1984.
Ten Sales From One Article Idea: The Process and Correspondence, 1982.

Audio Cassettes series:

Before You Write Your Nonfiction Book . . ., 1985.
How To Sell 75% of Your Freelance Writing, 1986.
How To Speak or Write an Idea Into a Windfall, 1985.
How To Set Up and Market Your Own Seminar, 1986.
   (plus eight single tapes listed on the last page of this book)

About Articles/Books:

Appelbaum/Evans, *How To Get Happily Published*, New American Library/ Plume.

Bell, Herbert, *How To Get Your Book Published: An Insider's Guide*, Writer's Digest Books.

Gross, Ronald, *The Independent Scholar's Handbook, How to Turn Your Interest in any Subject into Expertise*, Addison-Wesley Publishing Co.

Horowitz, Lois, *Knowing Where To Look, The Ultimate Guide to Research*, Writer's Digest Books.

Hull, Raymond, *How To Write How-To Books and Articles*, Writer's Digest Books.

Kremer, John, *101 Ways to Market Your Books, for Publishers and Authors*, Ad-Lib
     Publications.
Poynter/Bingham, *Is There a Book Inside You?*, Para Publishing.

About Self-Publishing:

Bodian, Nat G., *Book Marketing Handbook* (volumes 1 & 2), Bowker.
Kremer, John, *Book Marketing Made Easier*, Ad-Lib Publications.
Kremer, John, *The Independent Publisher's Bookshelf*, Ad-Lib Publications.
Poynter, Dan, *The Self-Publishing Manual*, Para Publishing.
Ross, Marilyn and Tom, *The Complete Guide to Self-Publishing*, Writer's Digest
     Books.

About Seminars/Speaking:

Bower, Sharon Anthony, *Painless Public Speaking*, Prentice-Hall.
Dutton, John, *How To Be An Outstanding Speaker*, Life Skills Publishing.
Fletcher, Leon, *How To Speak Like a Pro*, Ballantine Books.
Lant, Jeffrey, *Money Talks*, JLA Publications.
Linver, Sandy, *Speak Easy*, Simon and Schuster.
Murray, Sheila, *How to Organize and Manage a Seminar*, Prentice-Hall.
Shenson, Howard, *How To Create and Market a Successful Seminar or Workshop*,
     Bermont Books.

Other:

Hudson, Howard Penn, *Publishing Newsletters*, Charles Scribner's Sons.
Lant, Jeffrey, *The Unabashed Self-Promoter's Guide*, JLA Publications.

INDEX

Also available from
COMMUNICATION UNLIMITED

Title	BOOKS	Price
Empire-Building by Writing and Speaking (paper)		$ 12.95
Empire-Building by Writing and Speaking (cloth)		15.95
Query Letters/Cover Letters (paper)		9.95
Speaking For Money (paper)		9.95
Speaking For Money (cloth)		12.95
How To Sell 75% of Your Freelance Writing (paper)		9.95
How To Sell 75% of Your Freelance Writing (cloth)		12.95

TAPES

(Series, with workbooks)

How To Sell 75% of Your Freelance Writing (3 60-minute tapes)		39.95
Writing Travel Articles That Sell (3 tapes)		39.95
Writing Comedy Greeting Cards That Sell (2 tapes)		24.95
Before You Write Your Nonfiction Book . . . (3 tapes)		39.95
How To Set Up and Market Your Own Seminar (3 tapes)		44.95
How To Write or Speak an Idea Into a Windfall (3 tapes)		44.95

(Single 60-minute tapes)

Finding Ideas for Articles That Sell		9.95
Research: Finding Facts, Quotes, and Anecdotes		9.95
How To Be Quoted (Almost) All the Time		9.95
Back-of-the-Room Sales		9.95
Producing and Selling Your Audio Cassettes		9.95
Selling Your Product (and Others') by Mail Order		9.95
Creating, Selling, and Using Your Own Mailing List		9.95

Tax: California residents, add 6% sales tax
Shipping: $1, first book, tape, or series; 50 cents each additional
$2.50 maximum

☐ Please send information about new products!

COMMUNICATION UNLIMITED
P.O. Box 1001
Carpinteria, CA 93013